Employment Contract Manual

Desmond Payne and Keith Mackenzie

Gower

Published by
Gower Publishing Company Limited,
Gower House,
Croft Road,
Aldershot,
Hants GU11 3HR,
England

Gower Publishing Company,
Old Post Road,
Brookfield,
Vermont 05036,
U.S.A.

The information and interpretations contained in this publication are the opinions of the authors. A court is the only authority that can give a definitive decision on a point of law or interpret the facts of a particular case.

The authors accept no liability for loss or consequential damage arising from the use of any information contained in this publication.

British Library Cataloguing in Publication Data

Payne, Desmond
    Employment contract manual
    1. Labour contract—Great Britain
    I. Title II. Mackenzie, Keith
    344.106′24   KD3096

Library of Congress Cataloguing in Publication Data

Payne, Desmond
    Employment contract manual

    Includes index.
    1. Labour contract—Great Britain. 2. Labour contract—Great Britain—Forms.
    I. Mackenzie, Keith. II. Title.
    KD1634.P39   1987   344.41′01891   86-33517

ISBN 0-566-02654-6

Printed and bound by
Dotesios (Printers) Ltd,
Bradford-on-Avon, Wiltshire

EMPLOYMENT CONTRACT MANUAL

Contents

Preface

This Manual is intended as an aid to personal officers and others who have responsibility for formulating contract documentation.

Part One provides models for the contract documentation itself; that is, statement of terms, contract of employment, fixed-term contract and agreement for services.

The model agreement for services is designed for those who provide services, but is included so that such persons, who are not strictly employees, can be given documentation which will help to ensure that their status as 'sub-contractors' is distinguished from that of true employees. Each of the other models—the statement of terms, contract of employment and fixed-term contract—is allied to a more detailed Rules Book which forms part of the contract of employment.

Part Two, the Rules Book, contains models, and where appropriate variations, of rules which are often needed to ensure that both employer and employee understand what their respective entitlements and obligations are. Because the rules of employment are the essence of the employment relationship, this part of the Manual is perhaps the most important.

Part Three provides practice notes which help to explain the law and good practice for each part of the contractual relationship.

Part Four contains a number of model letters which may be useful when certain important parts of the contract of employment need to be activated.

Part Five provides a summary of the rights, obligations and restrictions imposed by employment legislation on employers and employees.

Application

The Manual takes account of industrial relations law as it stands at the time of writing but it may be that common law will affect the rights of the parties. For example, an employee who does not have the right to complain to an industrial tribunal may have redress under common law.

For convenience this Manual includes many provisions which apply solely to non-manual workers. However, the contents are easily adaptable to the manual sector.

If a particular group of workers is covered by a Wage Council order or a collective agreement, care should be taken to ensure that any terms of an order or agreement are not modified when constructing new documentation. The primary document (statement or contract) could end with a provision which states: 'Any term or condition of the .... Order/Agreement that is different to any provision stated above or in the Employment Rules Book shall modify or replace that provision as appropriate'.

Check Service

A rule or a variation from this Manual can be used as it stands, or it may need modification, or, indeed, particular rules may have no relevance to your organisation. Furthermore, although the Manual contains most commonly used rules you may well have specialised needs which are not included in this general publication: for example, membership of medical insurance schemes etc.

Therefore, after you have originated or revised your contracts and rules you may like to have them checked. If so, the authors of this publication will examine your documentation and let you have their comments. A charge will be made for this service and details of costs may be obtained from: SIGMA Consultants Ltd, 25A Market Square, Bicester, Oxon. OX6 7AD.

Part One
Contract Documentation

Contents of Part One

Introduction

The law requires that every employee be given, within 13 weeks of engagement, a statement specifying the main terms and conditions of employment. Therefore, it is useful to check, from time to time, that every employee has received such a statement and if not to issue one immediately.

This section of the manual contains the following models:

- A statement which includes all of the statutory information that is required. As a statutory statement of terms is not in itself a contract of employment (see the Practice Notes, Sections 3.1 and 3.2) a signature of receipt by the employee is sufficient.
- A contract of employment which incorporates the statutory information. In this case, the contract needs to be signed by both parties.
- A fixed-term contract of employment.
- An agreement for services.

As you will see from the guidance notes it is suggested that the primary document (statement, contract) should be used as a vehicle for referring the employee to a rules book and for dealing with those variations which are specific to the individual employee.

1.1 Model statement of terms

Statement of particulars of the main terms and conditions of your employment including those specified by Section 1 of the Employment Protection (Consolidation) Act 1978

Employee:

1   Date of issue of statement:

2   Job title:

3   The date this employment began:

4   Your period of employment began:

5   Your rate of pay and pay-day is in accordance with your pay-slip and the employer's pay register.

6   Your normal working hours are stated in the Employment Rules Book.

7   Your entitlement to holiday, holiday pay, sick-pay and pension is stated in the Employment Rules Book.

8   The notice that you have to give and the notice that you are entitled to receive on termination of employment is stated in the Employment Rules Book.

9   If you have a grievance relating to the employment you must first raise the matter with the Supervisor and then follow the procedure laid down in the Employment Rules Book.

10 Disciplinary rules are contained in the Employment Rules Book.

Your terms and conditions of employment include all of the provisions of the Employment Rules Book, and all of the above matters are dealt with further in that document. A further and current copy of that document can be inspected on application to your Supervisor.

Changes to any of the terms or conditions contained in this statement or in the Employment Rules Book will be notified to you in writing. Enquiries regarding any such change must be made to your Supervisor within twenty-eight days of that notification.

Any provision stated above or any provision that is stated in any attached addendum that is different from a corresponding provision of the Employment Rules Book shall modify or replace as appropriate the provision of the Employment Rules Book.

Received by: Date:

Guidance notes on statement of terms

1   Enter the date the statement is given to the employee. This should be no more than 13 weeks after commencement of employment.
2   Enter job title. This should be a broad description of the job. A detailed job description is not required by law and can be restrictive.
3   Enter the date of commencement of employment with you.
4   If there is any previous employment, such as occurs on a change of ownership, enter that earlier date here; otherwise (or if there is any doubt) enter the same date as in 3 above.
5   Reference to pay-slips avoids having to update the statement each time the rate of pay changes.
6, 7, 8 and 9   If any of these items is in any way different for a particular employee, state that difference here. For example, you may need to replace the existing item 6 with:

Your normal working hours are whatever hours the needs of the job dictate.

Or, if the wording of a particular amendment is lengthy, you may remove the reference as shown and substitute:

See the attached addendum.

In this case it would be as well to add a final paragraph to the addendum:

This amends and supersedes the corresponding provision of the Employment Rules Book.

The device of having a statement of terms separate from a rules book may be thought to be more useful than having a complete document for each employee. In this way the statement will show the individual variances at a glance and will entail the storage of just one sheet for each employee rather than a lengthy booklet. In some employments the variation in terms between groups of employees may be so great that a rules book for each group will be justified.

Any change to the statement should be notified to the individual concerned. Any changes, whether to the statement itself or to the Employment Rules Book, should be agreed in writing with the employee.

A currently updated copy of the Employment Rules Book must be kept available for inspection by any employee who so requests.

The note included in the statement about the notification of changes does not give you the right to make a change but merely states the procedure for notification.

The statement of terms is a statutory requirement. It does no more in law than state the position as the employer sees it. If it is thought that a contract of employment would be more appropriate the model in 1.2 should be used.

See Practice Note 3.1.

1.2   Model contract of employment

Contract of Employment including those particulars specified by Section 1 of the Employment Protection (Consolidation) Act 1978

between   (hereinafter called the Employee)

and   (hereinafter called the Company)

1   Dated:

2   The Employee's job title is:

3   The date employment under this contract began:

4   The period of employment began:

5   The Employee's rate of pay and pay-day is shown in the Company's pay register.

6   The Employee's normal working hours are stated in the Employment Rules Book.

7   Entitlement to holiday, holiday pay, sick-pay and pension is stated in the Employment Rules Book.

8   The notice that has to be given by both parties is stated in the Employment Rules Book.

9   If the Employee has a grievance relating to the employment, that grievance must first be raised with the Supervisor and thereafter the procedure laid down in the Employment Rules Book must be followed.

10 Disciplinary rules are stated in the Employment Rules Book.

The terms of this contract include all of the provisions of the Employment Rules Book and many of the above matters are dealt with further in that document. A further and current copy of that document can be inspected on application to the Supervisor.

Changes to any of the terms or conditions contained in this contract or in the Employment Rules Book will be notified in writing and any enquiry regarding any such change must be made within twenty-eight days of that notification.

Any provision stated above or any provision that is stated in any attached addendum that is different to a corresponding provision of the Employment Rules Book shall modify or replace as appropriate the provision of the Employment Rules Book.

Signed by the Employee: Date:

Signed for the Company: Date: *# Rule book After.*

Guidance notes on contract of employment

1 Enter the date the contract is given to the employee.
2 Enter job title. This should be a broad description of the job. A detailed job description is not required by law and can be restrictive.
3 Enter the date of commencement of employment with you.
4 If there is any previous employment, such as occurs on a change of ownership, enter that earlier date here; otherwise, or if there is any doubt, enter the same date as in 3 above.
5 Reference to pay-slips avoids having to update the contract each time the rate of pay changes.
6, 7, 8 and 9   If any of these items is in any way different for a particular employee state that difference here. For example, you may need to replace the existing item 6 with:

Your normal working hours are whatever hours the needs of the job dictate.

Or, if the wording of a particular amendment is lengthy, you may remove the reference as shown and substitute:

See the attached addendum.

In this case it would be as well to add a final paragraph to the addendum:

This amends and supersedes the corresponding provision of the Employment Rules Book.

The device of having a contract separate from a rules book may be thought to be more useful than having a complete document for each employee. In this way the contract will show the individual variances at a glance and will entail the storage of just one sheet for each employee rather than a lengthy booklet. In some employments the variation in terms between groups of employees may be so great that a rules book for each group will be justified.

Any change to the contract should be notified to the individual concerned. Any changes, whether to the contract itself or to the Employment Rules Book, should be agreed in writing with the employee.

A currently updated copy of the Employment Rules Book must be kept available for inspection by any employee who so requests.

The note included in the contract about the notification of changes does not give you the right to make a change but merely states the procedure for notification.

Unlike a statement of terms, a contract of employment is agreed between employer and employee to be binding upon both parties. If it is felt that a simple statutory statement of terms would be more appropriate the model in 1.1 should be used.

See Practice Note 3.2.

1.3 Model fixed-term contract of employment

Fixed-term Contract of Employment

between   (hereinafter called the Employee)

and   (hereinafter called the Company)

for the period commencing: and ending:

1 The Employee's job title is:

2 The Employee's rate of pay and pay-day is shown on the Employee's pay-slip and as recorded in the Company's pay register.

3 The Employee's normal working hours are stated in the Employment Rules Book.

4 Entitlement to holiday, holiday pay, sick-pay and pension is stated in the Employment Rules Book.

5 If the Employee has a grievance relating to the employment, that grievance must first be raised with the Supervisor and thereafter the procedure laid down in the Employment Rules Book must be followed.

6 At the expiry of this contract the Employee shall not be entitled to any redundancy payment nor entitlement to make claim for compensation for unfair dismissal under the provisions of any statute.

7 This contract incorporates all of the provisions of the Employment Rules Book except any such provisions which provide for termination of employment which are not in accord with the fixed-term provisions of this contract.

8 Any provision stated above or any provision that is stated in any attached addendum that is different from a corresponding provision of the Employment Rules Book shall modify or replace as appropriate the provision of the Employment Rules Book.

Signed by the Employee: Date:

Signed for the Company: Date:

Guidance notes on fixed-term contract of employment

A fixed-term contract of employment can be for any period which the parties to the contract, employer and employee, agree upon.

However, the parties cannot agree that the employee shall forego the right to redundancy pay or the right to complain of unfair dismissal under any fixed term short of one full year. Therefore, if a fixed-term contract short of a full year is agreed upon, the reference under item 8 should be deleted. These exclusions in respect of redundancy pay and unfair dismissal cannot be incorporated into any contract except that which is for a fixed term as above. Nor do these exclusions operate where there is a termination for a reason other than the mere expiry of the contract.

Where the employment is renewed under another contract the period of the fixed term will normally be continuous with that of the succeeding contract.

The main consideration relating to fixed-term contracts is that the period must have a stated commencement and concluding date (albeit that the employment may subsequently be continued). Consequently, the unilateral termination of the contract short of its full term would be actionable with a liability for compensation and/or damages unless it could be shown that a party was in fundamental breach of the contract, or that the contract was no longer capable of being performed.

(Note: An employee engaged on a fixed-term contract of three months or less has no entitlement to guaranteed pay if laid off or put on to short-time working.)

See also the guidance notes on statement of terms (p. 5).

See Practice Note 3.2.

1.4 Model agreement for services

Agreement for Services

This Agreement is made the   day of   19   between

whose head office is at
(hereinafter called the Company) of the one part and

(hereinafter called the Contractor) of the other part.

Whereas by a letter dated   19   the Contractor offered to make his services available to the Company to advise the Company on such aspects of its business as the Company may from time to time require the Company agreed to accept such offer on and subject to the terms and conditions set out in this Agreement.

Whereby it is agreed as follows:

Section 1—Period

1.01   The service provided by the Contractor to the Company shall be for a period commencing on and terminating on   but this period may be terminated earlier in accordance with the provisions of section 5 of this Agreement.

Section 2—Services

2.01   During the continuance of this Agreement the Contractor shall advise the Company on such aspects of its business as the Company may from time to time require.

2.02   During the continuance of this Agreement the Contractor shall devote such time, attention and abilities to meeting the Company's requirements referred to in clause 2.01 above as may be necessary to provide the Company with such services in the United Kingdom and in such other country or countries as the Company may require hereunder.

2.03   During the continuance of this Agreement the Contractor shall not work for any other person or business or government or any other body of whatsoever nature other than the Company in any connection whatsoever without the prior written approval of the Company.

Section 3—Payment

3.01 In consideration of services rendered by the Contractor hereunder the Company shall pay to the Contractor during the continuance of this Agreement a fee of   payable as follows:

Date: Payment:

3.02 Each instalment of the fee payable by the Company to the Contractor shall be paid to the Contractor in pounds sterling.

3.03 The Company shall reimburse to the Contractor all reasonable expenses properly incurred by the Contractor in carrying out the services under this Agreement provided first that all proposed travelling schedules shall before being undertaken be approved by the Company and secondly that all such expenses shall be properly vouched by written evidence where reasonably procurable.

Section 4—Secrecy

4.01 The Contractor shall not (except in the proper execution of services hereunder) during, or after the termination of, this Agreement either directly or indirectly disclose to any person or undertaking whatsoever any information relating to the Company or its business or projects of which the Contractor is now or may hereafter become possessed.

Section 5—Termination

5.01 Upon the happening of any of the following events the Company shall be entitled summarily to terminate this Agreement without notice and without making any payment to the Contractor other than for services already rendered:

(a) if the contractor shall be guilty of serious misconduct or any breach or non-observance of the terms of this Agreement; or

(b) if the Contractor shall neglect, fail, refuse or shall for any reason be unable to provide the services under this Agreement.

Section 6—PAYE and national insurance contribution indemnity

6.01 The Contractor represents that during the continuance of this Agreement the Company is not required to deduct from payments made to the Contractor under the terms of this Agreement any income tax or national insurance contribution. If however it is determined at any time either during or after the termination of this Agreement that the Company is liable for any such payments then the Contractor will reimburse to the Company any such liability.

Section 7—Delivering up documents

7.01 The Contractor or the Contractor's personal representative shall upon the termination of this Agreement deliver up to the Company all correspondence, documents, specifications, papers and property belonging to the Company which may be in the Contractor's possession or under the Contractor's control and shall keep no copies of or extracts from these.

Section 8—Communications

8.01 Any communications to be given hereunder shall be addressed:

(a) in the case of the Company to:

(b) in the case of the Contractor to:

or to such other address as either party may notify to the other by not less than ten days prior notice in writing.

Section 9—Law

9.01 This Agreement shall be governed and construed in accordance with English law.

As witness the hands of the parties hereto or their duly authorised representatives the day and year first above written.

By the Company

By the Contractor

See Practice Note 3.3.

1.5   Variations

If a statement or contract of employment is used without reference to a separate rules book you should ensure that the statement or contract includes all of the required legislative information. You may wish to take the wording of this, or your own adaptations, from Part 2—the model rules. This should replace the references to the Employment Rules Book.

In addition, the final paragraphs 1 and 3 of the statement and contract would need to be deleted and paragraph 2 modified. Any other provision, perhaps adapted from the model rules in Part 2, could be inserted as additional paragraphs.

The fixed-term contract of employment (1.3) model also could be similarly amended.

The Agreement for Services (1.4) is a generalised model. The circumstances in which such an agreement could be of use are so varied that it would be impossible to provide a model which would meet every need. The subject of the Agreement could possibly be a consultant or a manual worker, or a gang or partnership, etc, and their terms would all have to be appropriately different. But whatever the form of the Agreement it is important that there should be no confusion between the status of work 'for services' (sub-contract) and work 'of service' (employment).

Part Two
Employment Rules Book

Contents of Part Two

Introduction

An Employment Rules Book or Staff Handbook should set out as fully as possible all the contractual rights and obligations of the employer and employee.

The model rules contained in this part of the manual covers all those rules most usually needed by employers; and in some cases variations are provided which show alternative ways of dealing with a particular rule.

It will, of course, be necessary for the user to adjust many of the rules to meet specific requirements, and some rules may not be needed at all. Also, some of the terminology, for example Supervisor, Head of Department, Personnel Department, etc., may need alteration.

It is best to make the rules book standard for all employees, or all employees within a category. Clearly, variations will be needed for certain employees, for example job titles cannot be identical and it may be that a variation will be necessary in the hours of work. The best way to cope with such individual variations is to specify the difference in the primary document (the statement of terms, etc.) rather than to alter the rules book for one employee.

Many companies call the rules book a Staff Handbook, however the name given to it is not important provided that it is indicative of its purpose and that the same name is used throughout.

As employment law and practice is often subject to change, the rules book should be produced in a form which is easily amendable. It may, for example, be stored on a word processor; or the final draft photocopied. This approach not only facilitates updating but is cost effective since altering printed matter is expensive.

The rules should be examined at least once a year to keep them in line with current law and practice. A useful device to ensure that accurate records are kept of when amendments have been made is to print the date of issue at the foot of each page, e.g. 1/87. Thus, a page can be withdrawn and a new one issued in substitution, showing the month and year of issue.

There are two main ways in which new rules can be introduced. The first is to adopt the 'gradualist' approach, that is to issue the new rules to new employees as they commence employment, leaving existing employees with their current contracts. The disadvantage with this method is that different rules will operate for different employees. The second approach is to ask all employees to accept new contracts. If this approach is adopted some inducement may have to be offered to gain acceptance, such as making a pay increase dependent upon consent. A useful device is to revise the rules annually, linking their reissue with the annual pay award.

2.1 Foreword

All employees of the Company are given a copy of this Rules Book so that they may more easily understand the rules governing their employment.

Everyone employed by the Company is a member of the team and each employee has a part to play if the Company is to maintain job security. In order that we may all contribute to the team success it is essential that we both know and observe the rules governing our day-to-day activities.

These rules are part of your contract of employment. Good standards of conduct and work-performance are essential to the maintenance of employment and the continued improvement of employee benefits and it is therefore in your interest to read and understand these rules.

If you mislay your copy of these rules, or if there is any matter which is not clear, please refer to your Supervisor or to the Personnel Department.

Any amendment to the rules will be notified to you and it is your responsibility to update your copy.

It is your responsibility to notify the Company immediately of any change in your personal circumstances, such as address, marital status, and so on.

This Rules Book must be returned to the Personnel Department on leaving the Company's employment.

Notes:
1   In this Rules Book 'Supervisor' means the person in the company to whom you are directly responsible.
2   A 'Head of Department' is a person who supervises a division, department or section of employees, as appropriate.
3   The use of the masculine pronoun throughout this Rules Book includes the feminine as appropriate.
4   Each part of this Rules Book forms part of your contract of employment and should therefore be read with care.

See Practice Note 3.4.

2.2   Hours of work

Unless otherwise specified in your statement of terms, normal office working hours are from 9.00 a.m. to 5.00 p.m., including one hour for lunch, Monday to Friday inclusive, that is a total of 35 working hours in each week.

In certain areas, especially where shift arrangements operate, the actual hours of work may be different to those above as specified at commencement of employment.

You are entitled to one hour for lunch to be taken at a time specified by your Head of Department between the hours of 11.30 a.m. and 3.00 p.m.

At commencement and completion of working hours you must, unless you have written exemption, record your arrival and leaving in the Attendance Book in the approved form and you must state any reason for late arrival or early leaving.

The need to work overtime will be kept to a minimum but there may be occasions when it is necessary for you to work overtime. In that event you will be given as much notice as is possible.

Overtime may only be worked with the prior approval of your Head of Department.

When overtime is worked this must be indicated in the Attendance Book with the signature of your Head of Department or Supervisor.

You will be eligible for overtime payment if you are below the level of Assistant Manager.

The minimum overtime that will be paid in any one day is half an hour of continuous overtime.

Payment for overtime is for each full half-hour at the rate of time-and-a-half for weekdays and Saturdays and double-time for Sundays and statutory holidays, and will be paid one month in arrears.

Overtime rates are based on your annual basic salary and do not take into account additional payments such as shift payments etc.

Time off in lieu of overtime worked can only be allowed in exceptional circumstances as authorised by your Head of Department.

Variations

There may be some employees for whom it is not practicable to specify working hours which are fixed; for example, many executives work different hours each week, or even each day, according to the dictates of the job, particularly where the job entails a lot of travelling.

In those cases it probably will be sensible to say that:

19

> The normal hours of work are whatever reasonable hours the needs of the job dictate.

In other cases a better wording might be:

> The normal working hours are whatever hours are needed for the satisfactory completion of the job in hand.

Whatever form is adopted, if definite hours are not specified in terms of time then it is essential that the pay position is clarified; that is, whether the salary is all-embracing of the hours worked or whether there is extra pay for extra hours.

Where such an alternative is used which is at variance with the general position of other employees it may be that this variance is incorporated into the appropriate contract documentation of the individual rather than having an amendment to the rules book.

Clearly, an employer who wishes to have control over absenteeism and poor timekeeping needs to have good records. The usual methods are to require the employee to record arrival and perhaps departure in an attendance book or by use of a time-clock. It may be that some grades of employees will be exempt from such a recording system. This may be stated in the rules book but it is probably better done in the statement of terms.

A negative recording system is used by some companies. That is, only those employees who arrive late are required to sign in. This has the advantage of impressing upon the employee the fact of being late. However, it does require that someone must be placed to ensure that latecomers do in fact sign in.

Where an attendance recording system is not in use it may be that overtime will have to be controlled by use of overtime forms completed by the Head of Department. If the overtime system requires the employee to submit an overtime claim form it would be useful to have a provision in the rules such as:

> Properly completed overtime claim forms must be returned to the Personnel Department by the first working day of the month in respect of overtime worked during the previous month.

A variation adopted by some companies is:

> If an employee is required to work on a rest-day or bank holiday a reasonable time will be allowed for travel to and from work to be included for overtime pay.

See Practice Note 3.5.

2.3   Holidays

The holiday year begins on the first day of March and ends on the last day of February.
Statutory holidays are as promulgated by Government.
The annual paid leave entitlement is as follows (calculated at the normal rate of pay):

- Managers and above — ... working days
- Assistant and Deputy Managers — ... working days
- All other employees — ... working days
  in a holiday year.

Where employment is commenced during the holiday year the above entitlement will be reduced by one-twelfth for each complete month in the holiday year preceding the month of commencement, rounded up to one full day. This provision is amended by any agreement made before employment commenced.

Where employment is terminated during the holiday year the above entitlement will be reduced by one-twelfth for each complete month in the holiday year following the month of termination, rounded up to one full day. No reduction will be made for holiday taken prior to termination that is in excess of this entitlement.

The timing of annual leave is subject to the prior approval of your Supervisor and it is advisable to request your leave dates well in advance. Because of seasonal or other demands it may not be possible to allow you to take leave at certain times.

Leave entitlement does not accrue from one holiday year to another except where prior consent is given in exceptional circumstances by your Head of Department.

Where there is a leave entitlement outstanding at termination of employment a payment in lieu will be made at the daily pay rate mentioned in section 2.5 on Remuneration.

At least two holiday weeks must be taken together but the special approval of your Head of Department is required for any holiday period exceeding two weeks.

If your entitlement increases because of promotion the extra entitlement is allowed in the holiday year in which that promotion occurs.

For employees below manager level the entitlement increases by one day for each completed period of five years of continuous employment subject to a maximum of twenty-five working days.

Leave is not normally allowable during the period of termination notice.

Time off for religious observance must be taken from annual leave and will be subject to the approval of your Supervisor.

Where either statutory or annual holiday is worked an extra payment will be made for each day so worked calculated as set out in section 2.5 on Remuneration.

Where it is agreed that holiday shall be taken in lieu of any that is worked there shall be no extra payment.

No additional allowance of either payment or holiday is allowed for sickness at any statutory or annual holiday time.

Variations

There must, of course, be variations for the needs of individual companies. For example, the holiday year may run with the calendar year, the amount of leave entitlement and the grades of staff and so on may be different.

It may be that you will wish to exclude or limit the probationer's holiday entitlement. If so, that may be better included under the Probation heading (see section 2.4).

You may also wish to clarify the position where an employee is taken sick during holiday. A variation on this might be:

No additional holiday will be allowed to compensate for incapacity through sickness or injury during a holiday period.

Another variation which may be useful is some formula for the booking of holidays. Perhaps along the lines of first-come takes precedence, or senior staff take precedence, etc.

If difficulties are encountered with employees who overstay holiday periods it may be useful to incorporate some rule about this. For example:

Holiday pay entitlement is dependent upon the employee being at work during all normal hours on the normal working day preceding and on the normal working day following the holiday.

and, perhaps, adding:

In cases where an employee is absent from work on one of the days specified in the previous paragraph, management may at its discretion withhold part or all of the holiday pay otherwise due to that employee.

It has been held in one appeal case that it was proper to have a contract provision whereby employment was automatically terminated by non-attendance on the day of due return. However, it appears that this decision may not hold good in other cases.

Most companies choose to forbid the accrual of holiday entitlement from one year to another except in compassionate cases, or where management has approved the holiday carry-forward because of an exceptional work-load, etc. However, there are companies who allow a limited carry-forward, such as:

An employee may carry forward from one holiday year to the next a maximum of ... days' holiday.

Similarly, because of problems of proof, most companies do not make an allowance for additional holiday or payment for holiday-time sickness. A small number of companies do make such an allowance as follows:

An employee who is sick during a period of annual leave and who can provide a doctor's certificate may, at the sole discretion of management, be granted a further leave entitlement for the whole or part of the sickness period to be taken at a time specified by management.

See Practice Note 3.6.

22

2.4   Probation

On joining the Company you are required to serve a probationary period of one year. On satisfactory completion of this period you will be appointed to the permanent staff and this will be confirmed in writing. Progress reports will be made on you at intervals during this probationary period. If at any time during that period it is decided by management that you do not meet the requirements of the Company your employment will be terminated with due notice.

Variations

A variation which does not relate the probationary period to work-performance could be stated as follows:

On joining the Company you will become entitled to certain benefits as specified in the Employment Rules Book. Some of these benefits are dependent upon a period of employment. The granting of such benefits does not imply that any particular standard of work-performance has been achieved.

This variation may be included as an alternative to a work-performance probationary rule or it may be added to such a rule. (You may wish to list any benefits which are service-dependent, such as entry to the pension scheme.)

An appraisal variation could be:

On joining the Company, appraisals of performance will be taken into consideration after periods of one, three, six and nine months and thereafter at annual intervals. Some benefits may accrue after initial intervals of employment but are not to be taken as acceptance of satisfactory performance. If at any time during the first twelve months it is decided by management that your performance does not meet the requirements of the Company your employment will be terminated with due notice.

You may also wish to add:

The performance of each employee is appraised by the Supervisor on an annual basis. This provides an opportunity for you and your Supervisor to discuss your past performance, your strengths and any areas for improvement. A copy of your appraisal form is kept on record and may be seen at any reasonable time on application.

See Practice Note 3.7.

2.5 Remuneration

Your salary will be paid by bank transfer normally on the last working Wednesday in each month. At the same time you will be issued with a pay-slip which will show gross pay, any deductions and the net amount credited to your account.

Your monthly pay is one-twelfth of your annual basic salary rate.

Any payments which fall to be calculated on a daily rate, such as where you commence or leave employment during a month, will be based on 1/260th of annual basic salary.

Where in any month, such as at commencement of employment, the amount due to you is less than one-quarter of a normal month's salary that payment may be held over for payment in the succeeding month (except that no payment shall be held over for more than one month).

Variations

You may wish to include the following variations:

- Where a deduction from pay is required that cannot be implemented in the month in which it falls due for deduction that sum shall be deducted from the pay due in the month immediately following. Where no further money is due to that employee it shall be repaid by the employee to the Company.
- Your salary will be paid by bank transfer normally on the .... day of each month. Where this day falls at a weekend or a statutory holiday, the pay-day will be the nearest working day prior to the normal pay-day.
- Pay statements will be issued when salary is transferred. Statements for employees on leave or absent for other reasons will be retained by the Personnel Department until such time as the employee collects the statement or authorises some other person, in writing, to collect.
- Luncheon vouchers are provided for employees at the rate of one voucher to the value of ... for each day worked. Vouchers are not provided for non-work days such as holidays, sickness or other forms of absence.
- Authorised expenses properly incurred in the performance of Company duties will be reimbursed on production of valid receipts. Reimbursement will be made within ... days/for claims submitted earlier than ... days prior to a pay-day, on that pay-day[*].

Note:
* Delete as applicable.

See Practice Note 3.8.

2.6 Salary policy

All salaries are reviewed annually.

The Company operates a merit-based salary policy which takes account of the personal contribution made by the individual employee. An annual assessment of performance is made. The Company also takes account of matched jobs in similar organisations.

Economic factors require that there can be no annual standard increases in salary, either generally or for the particular employee.

Where management deems that a particular employee is being paid above the rate which is either compatible with other similar Company employees or with similar employment external to the Company the salary of that employee will be held at the current level or will be increased at a reduced level until the position is regularised. The employee will be notified of the duration of this period.

Where management deems that an employee is to receive no increase in salary or an increase smaller than would otherwise be paid because of a performance assessment, the employee will be told and will be invited to discuss the matter with a senior manager.

Any employee affected by this policy is reminded that any grievance arising from the policy must be taken up through the normal grievance procedure in which case a further review of that person's salary will be undertaken before the grievance is processed through the procedure.

2.7 Job title

Your job title conveys a generalised indication of your position. It is not intended to be restrictive and you may at times be required to undertake duties within your capabilities beyond the confines of your usual job.

Variations

If you have a general scheme of job descriptions you may wish to vary this provision as follows:

The work that you are required to do is governed by a job description. A schedule of job descriptions is appended, the appropriate provisions of which apply to you/is indicated on your Statement of Terms[*] and forms part of your contract of employment.

If a job description applies to the individual and not the generality of employees it may be preferable to state it against the item 'Job Title' in the statement or contract or in an appendix.

You may prefer an alternative:

Your job title is a broad indication of the work you are required to do. However, you may be required to undertake other duties, particularly when others are absent from work. No job title or job description can be regarded as a precise specification of duties but should be seen as a guide to main responsibilities.

Note:
* Delete as applicable.

See Practice Note 3.9.

2.8 Place of employment

You may be required at any time with reasonable notice to transfer to any other location within the United Kingdom if the necessity arises. In such cases all expenses directly attributable to the transfer will be refunded to you except for any difference in house prices or accommodation costs.

You may be required at any time and without notice to transfer from one department to another within the Company.

These rights of transfer do not allow alteration to your job or to your pay or other conditions of employment.

Variations

It is important to specify an area or distance which is relevant to the needs of the business:

Employees in the category of [service engineers, erectors, etc.] shall work on any site as directed within the area of/the radius of/... miles/kilometres of home measured in a straight line[*].

A provision with no such specification or with an inappropriate specification could be invalid.

The following variation is for use for employees required to travel abroad or who are seconded abroad temporarily:

For the purposes of any law governing employment your normal place of employment shall be Great Britain [and Northern Ireland] and this definition is not modified by any temporary periods worked elsewhere.

A variation may be included for employees on temporary secondment from abroad:

You are employed on temporary secondment from [France etc.] and for the purposes of employment law your normal place of employment shall be [France etc.]. All of the provisions of the Statement of Terms/Contract of Employment[*] and the related Employment Rules Book shall apply to you except where they provide a right or obligation which is only relevant to employees normally employed in Great Britain [and Northern Ireland].

An employer whose business requires that employees work for other businesses, say service engineers who carry out work on a client's premises, may encounter difficulties if that client refuses to allow an individual to work at his premises. Such an employer could usefully include such a rule as:

Where the employee is under the control, instruction or direction of a client or is required to work on the site of or at a location designated by that client; and if that client requires the termination of service by that employee for whatsoever reason or for no reason, the Company shall examine the possibility of transferring the employee to another suitable place of work. If such transfer is not possible the Company shall examine the possibility of providing suitable alternative employment. Such transfer or alternative employment obligations shall not apply in cases where the reason for termination of service is shown to be because of any misconduct on the part of the employee. If transfer or offer of alternative employment is not possible the employee's employment with the Company shall be terminated for the substantial reason of the client's requirement.

Note:
* Delete as applicable.

See Practice Note 3.10.

2.9 Maternity

An employee with sufficient qualifying service has a statutory right to certain maternity pay. In addition she is entitled to take time off work for the confinement and beyond and time off for antenatal care.

Such an employee will have obligations of notification and should therefore contact her Supervisor at an early date during her pregnancy for full details.

Variations

The contract of employment is not normally the place for advising employees of their statutory rights. Moreover, statements by employers which are interpretations of the law can create unnecessary difficulties. Therefore the model rule is limited to a brief reminder. Nevertheless, there may be some companies who wish to be more informative, as:

> Subject to the provisions of the relevant statutes, an employee who has completed two years of continuous employment with the Company by the start of the eleventh week before the expected week of her confinement has the right to certain maternity pay and a further right to take time off work and to return to her job (or a suitable alternative job) up to twenty-nine weeks after confinement.
>
> Such an employee must produce a certificate from a registered medical practitioner or a certified midwife stating the expected week of her confinement.
>
> An employee who does not so wish to return to work after her confinement should notify the Company.
>
> An employee undergoing antenatal care has a right to take time off to attend for that care.
>
> The rate of maternity pay and other conditions which attach to both paid and unpaid maternity leave and antenatal time off are governed by statute and the employee should apply to the Personnel Department at an early date for further information.

See Practice Note 3.11.

Employment Contract Manual

Supplement October 1987

Please note that sections 2.9 (page 29) and 3.11 (page 91) should be amended as shown.

2.9 Maternity

An employee who has been continuously employed for not less than two years at the beginning of the eleventh week before the expected week of her confinement has rights to certain maternity pay. In addition she is entitled to take time off work for the confinement and beyond and time off for antenatal care.

Such an employee will have obligations of notification and should therefore contact her Supervisor at an early date for full details.

Variations

The contract of employment is not normally the place for advising employees of their statutory rights. Moreover, statements by employers which are interpretations of the law can create unnecessary difficulties. Therefore, the model rule is limited to a brief reminder. Nevertheless, there may be some companies who wish to be more informative, as:

Subject to the provisions of the relevant statutes, an employee who has completed two years of continuous employment with the Company by the start of the eleventh week before the expected week of her confinement has the right to maternity pay for a period of up to six weeks and a further right to take time off work and to return to her job (or a suitable alternative job) up to twenty-nine weeks after confinement.

Such an employee must produce a certificate from a registered medical practitioner or a certified midwife stating the expected week of her confinement.

An employee who does not so wish to return to work after her confinement should notify the Company.

An employee undergoing antenatal care has a right to take time off to attend for that care.

The rate of maternity pay and other conditions which attach to both paid and unpaid maternity leave and antenatal time off are governed by statute and the employee should apply to the Personnel Department at an early date for further information.

See Practice Note 3.11.

2.10   Attendance

Compassionate leave may be granted on application to your Supervisor depending on the reason for the request and may be paid or not as management deems appropriate. Such leave is normally only allowable in cases of sickness or bereavement of a close relative or for an employee getting married.

A male employee whose wife or common law wife is expecting a baby will be entitled to extra leave allowance of three days to be taken at the time of confinement, or at a later agreed time if the confinement occurs during annual holiday.

A half-day with pay is allowed for Christmas shopping to be taken at a time approved by your Supervisor.

The above allowances are not conditioned by length of service.

Attendance at work, at the proper times, is important to the maintenance of efficiency.

If you have need of leave of absence you should contact your Supervisor as early as possible so that if permission is granted arrangements can be made for your work to be covered where necessary. Leave of absence will normally only be granted in exceptional circumstances.

All unauthorised absence from work, including poor timekeeping, is recorded and will be taken into account when deciding such matters as promotion, employee benefits, redundancy selection and so on, and may lead to disciplinary action.

In the event of industrial action, adverse weather or any other similar occurrence that makes travel difficult, management may require selected personnel to take up accommodation near to the Company on weekdays for the duration of that difficulty. Accommodation and related costs will be met by the Company. In such an event other employees are required to make every reasonable effort to attend work as near normally as is possible and to report by telephone if attendance that day is not possible. All employees may be required to work unusual hours for the duration of such emergency.

Variations

It may be felt that reasons for approved absence should not be specified. That all absences, beyond those provided for by statute, should be discretionary. For example:

Compassionate leave may be granted on application to your Supervisor depending on the reason for the request, and may be paid or not as management deems appropriate. Each request will be examined and decided upon its merits and any leave that is granted should not be taken as any sort of precedent for other cases.

On the other hand, some companies do specify circumstances in which they will grant extra leave, such as paternity, death of a close relative, moving house, training with the auxiliary armed forces, etc.

The period of such leave may be discretionary or may be specified, for example:

- Moving house: One day of paid/unpaid[*] leave will be granted for the purpose of moving house. No more than one day will be allowed for this purpose in any one year.
- Auxiliary services: The Company may grant one week each year of paid/unpaid[*] leave in addition to normal leave entitlement for employees undergoing training with one of the armed service auxiliary forces. Applications for such leave must be made at the earliest possible time and must be accompanied by the appropriate service documents. This entitlement is subject to the organisational needs of the Company.

Note:
* Delete as applicable.

See Practice Note 3.12.

2.11   Statutory time off

You have the right to leave of absence in the following circumstances:

- Jury service (and in certain circumstances, court attendance).

You should advise the Personnel Department as soon as possible if you are:

- A justice of the peace.
- A member of a local authority.
- A member of a statutory tribunal.
- A member of a Health Authority or Board.
- A member of the governing body of certain schools or colleges.
- A member of a water authority or river board.

These rights are subject to reasonability and you must therefore notify the Personnel Department as soon as possible to obtain the required leave of absence.

Paid leave of absence will be granted for the above reasons provided that you notify your Supervisor at the earliest possible date. This payment is subject to production by you of proof that you have claimed any loss-of-earnings allowance due to you, and any such allowances must be refunded by you to the Company.

Note: Other statutory time-off rights such as maternity leave are dealt with elsewhere in the Rules Book.

Variations

A company which has a recognition agreement with an independent trade union may wish to include something about the statutory rights of union officials or members to take time off work. The law on this subject is not simple and so it is recommended that an attempt to define those rights in the contract of employment should be avoided:

Certain officials of the recognised trade union have rights to take time off work for approved trade union duties and training which in some circumstances may be paid. There are also circumstances where the ordinary member may have the right to take time off work, unpaid, for some trade union activities. The rules governing these rights can be ascertained from the union or the Personnel Department. However, it is stressed that an application to take such time off must be made to the Personnel Department as early as possible.

These time-off rights do not extend to officials or members of unrecognised trade unions.

You may prefer a more simple rule for statutory time off:

If you require time off work for jury service or other statutory public duties you must notify the Personnel Department. You are required to claim from the relevant public body whatever expenses are allowed which must be notified to the Personnel Department for deduction from your pay. Failure to so claim or notify will result in an estimated sum being deducted.

See Practice Note 3.13.

2.12   Sickness and injury

If you are absent from work because of sickness or injury you must notify your Supervisor or Head of Department on the first day of absence, preferably by telephone, stating the reason for absence. If both those persons are unobtainable you must leave a message with the switchboard operator. If it is impossible for you to do so personally you must ensure that someone telephones on your behalf. Failure to do so will result in sick pay being withheld. [Para. 1]

If possible, you should also give your Supervisor an indication of when you expect to be able to return to work. [Para. 2]

Sickness absence of any duration must be supported by a certificate in the form approved by the Company. The employee must obtain that certificate from the Supervisor, and return it completed to the Supervisor immediately on return to work. During long-term absence the Company may post certificates to the employee for completion and immediate return. [Para. 3]

After seven consecutive days of absence you must submit a doctor's certificate in addition to Company certificates. [Para. 4]

For absence of more than seven consecutive days' duration that are not covered by a doctor's period certificate you must submit a final clearance certificate before resuming work. [Para. 5]

Periods not covered by properly submitted certificates will count as non-sickness absence and may be subject to disciplinary action. [Para. 6]

Submission of a certificate does not necessarily mean that there is an automatic entitlement to sick pay. [Para. 7]

If you hold a DHSS notice disqualifying you from statutory sick pay you must hand it to your Supervisor without delay. [Para. 8]

If you receive any sickness benefit direct from the State you must notify your Supervisor. [Para. 9]

The Company will pay sick leave at your normal basic salary rate for the following periods:

Length of continuous service	Maximum entitlement in any 12-month period
... days or more	... working days
... year or more	... working days
... years or more	... working days

There will be no additional holiday entitlement for sickness during holiday. [Para. 10]

34

Any sick-pay that is exceptionally granted shall not be taken as constituting a contractual obligation. [Para. 11]

Any statutory sick pay entitlement shall offset any sickness payment that is made as above. [Para. 12]

Wherever possible you should seek medical advice for illness or injury. In any event the Company requires you to see a doctor if the illness or injury is likely to cause an absence of more than three working days. [Para. 13]

It is important that if you contract, or are in contact with, a contagious or infectious disease your Supervisor must be notified at once. [Para. 14]

The Company may require you to consult a doctor of its choice during or after any period of sickness or injury absence. [Para. 15]

Sick-pay entitlement ceases when an employee reaches normal retirement age and upon cessation of employment with the Company. [Para. 16]

Variations

Paragraph 1 above which requires notification on the first day of absence is in line with the statutory sick pay provisions and should be retained. The operative word in the last sentence is 'withheld'. This does not necessarily mean that payment will not be made—it merely allows time to decide whether or not the absence was due to genuine sickness.

Paragraph 2, dealing with return to work, is not essential and may be omitted if desired.

Paragraph 3 is for use where the company operates its own self-certification scheme requiring certification for every sickness absence no matter how brief. This could be amended if desired to require company self-certification after, say, three days.

If the company has no certification scheme of its own and relies upon the statutory provisions entirely then paragraph 3 may be altered (deleting paragraph 4) to:

After three days of absence you must let the Company/Personnel Department[*] have sight of a statutory self-certificate (obtainable from your doctor) and after seven days of absence you must submit doctor's certificates in the normal way.

Paragraph 5 is optional but probably desirable.

Paragraph 6 provides a clear demarcation between sickness absence and unauthorised absence with the onus upon the employee to show that sickness was the reason for absence. However, this does not relieve the employer from the duty of making enquiries of the employee about reasons for absence if disciplinary action is contemplated on the ground of absenteeism.

Paragraph 7 is a mere statement of fact to cover the position where the employee's absence is so long that it runs out of entitlement to statutory or contractual sick pay.

Paragraphs 8 and 9 are intended to put the onus for notification of receipt of state benefit (which may affect either statutory or contractual sick pay benefit) upon the employee.

Obviously, contractual sick pay periods have to be adjusted to the contractual obligation of the individual company. If there is no obligation other than statutory sick pay this should be made clear, for example, in place of paragraphs 10 and 12 dealing with entitlement:

There is no sick pay except statutory sick pay.

The amendments consequential on this are to delete paragraph 16 dealing with entitlement at retirement age. All other paragraphs could stay.

Paragraph 11 allows for the exceptional circumstances where the company wishes to make a payment where it has no contractual obligation at all, or where it wishes to extend a payment period beyond its contractual limits.

Paragraph 13 is a useful reminder to the employee to see a doctor and is particularly necessary if there is no contractual sick-pay entitlement.

If an employee does report a contagious or infectious disease (see paragraph 14) then it is important to get a medical opinion about whether or not it is safe to allow the employee to continue at work. (Paragraph 15 could be invoked.)

Paragraph 15 requiring examination by a company-appointed doctor should be used only when there is any doubt about the sickness; undiscriminating use of this provision could lead to a feeling by the employee of harassment, and even a complaint of constructive dismissal.

Paragraph 16 provides an age limitation which, although not essential, may be thought to be useful.

Notes:
1   * Delete as applicable.
2   As is mentioned elsewhere in this Manual, the contract of employment is not normally the place to notify employees of their statutory rights. An attempt to reproduce the legislative provisions of statutory sick pay could be dangerous. Nor is it normally necessary to state qualifying days in the contract.

See Practice Note 3.14.

2.13   Medical examinations

All managers and above and all employees aged fifty and over may be required to undergo a medical examination. Except where there has been recent sickness, the employee will not normally be required to undergo such an examination at a greater frequency than two years.

2.14   Personal appearance

The Company requires all employees to conform to a standard of dress that is appropriate to the Company's business. Consequently, it is important to maintain a smart appearance during all working hours. Standards of personal appearance cannot be wholly specified in advance and must therefore be for the subjective judgement of management. Where any particular item of dress or appearance is considered by management to be inappropriate, that employee will be informed and will henceforth be required to adhere to the required standard.

The nature of an employee's work or work-location may have an effect in determining what is considered acceptable.

Whilst it is the Company's policy to apply equal standards of personal appearance to men and women there will be different applications, in particular:

- Male employees will not be permitted to wear ear-rings or other ear adornments.
- Male employees are required to wear a lounge suit and tie.
- Male employees will not be permitted to wear pullovers and cardigans.
- The wearing of jeans and other casuals will not be permitted.

Guidance on suitable appearance can be obtained from your Head of Department.

Variation

The Company requires employees to conform to standards of dress and appearance which are appropriate to their positions and client contact. It is not possible to lay down in advance specifications of dress and appearance and employees must therefore comply with any reasonable instruction in this respect.

See Practice Note 3.15.

2.15   Relationships

In cases where employees working in close proximity, or whose work requires mutual co-operation, form a close relationship which could have a detrimental effect upon that work or upon other employees then the Company may first examine the possibility of transfer, or an offer of alternative employment. If such transfer or offer is not practicable, employment may be terminated for that substantial reason. Such transfer, offer or termination shall be applied to the person in respect of whom, in the judgement of management, that action is likely to least harm the continuing interests of the Company.

See Practice Note 3.16.

2.16   General restrictions

During the period of your employment with the Company you must not engage in any other paid employment or carry out any trade, profession or business which is prejudicial to the interests of the Company.

Employees are forbidden to transact any business on their own account which may be business properly undertaken by the Company unless there has been prior written permission so to do.

No employee shall hold a directorship or any other business without the prior written permission of the Company.

No employee shall accept any gift from any outside person or organisation without declaring the nature of the gift and the circumstances in which it was given. If it is then the opinion of management that acceptance of the gift was inappropriate the employee shall dispose of it as directed by management.

Variations

An employer does not have the right to restrict an employee's outside interests which do not intrude into his working hours and which have no detrimental effect upon the employer's business.

It is difficult to specify every possible employee activity which might be detrimental to the employer. Therefore, a restrictive condition couched in general terms such as 'prejudicial to the interests of the Company' is likely to be sufficient. However, it may be thought that it would be useful to give some emphasis to certain matters, such as:

- Secondary employment or work is not allowed where it is likely to have an adverse effect upon your work-performance for the Company, particularly where such additional activities leave you tired or where they restrict your ability to fulfil your overtime obligations to the Company.
- Secondary employment must not involve use of the Company's property or resources or intrude upon working hours whether normal or overtime.

See Practice Note 3.17.

2.17   Confidentiality

You must not disclose to any unauthorised person any confidential information about the Company or any of its customers.

On termination of employment you must deliver to the Company any files, documents, other papers and property of every description within your possession or control belonging to the Company.

See Practice Note 3.17.

2.18 Lay-off and short-time working

It is the objective of the Company always to maintain full employment. Nevertheless, there may be times when this is not possible because of temporary difficulties.

The Company wishes to avoid being forced to dismiss employees in circumstances which may be of short duration. Therefore, in the event of a temporary cessation or diminution of work beyond the control of the Company, employees may be laid off or put on to short-time working to the extent and with the pay prescribed in the Employment Protection (Consolidation) Act 1978.

See Practice Note 3.18.

2.19   Pensions and retirement

Employees will normally be required to retire from employment with the Company at the age of 65.

There may be circumstances where for individuals this normal retirement age will be varied for business or compassionate reasons but such variations shall not be taken as amending the above normal retirement age.

Pension and other benefit rules that relate to retirement or death during service are stated in the Pension Rules Booklet a copy of which is provided and of which a further copy may be inspected on application to the Supervisor.

The Company is not contracted out of the State Earnings Related Pension Scheme.

Variations

It is a requirement of law that you state in the contract of employment whether or not you are contracted-out of the State Earnings Related Pension Scheme.

The age at which employees are required by an employer to retire is a matter for the employer, provided there is no discrimination between the sexes, but if the retirement age is different to that provided in the statute, that different age must be stated in the contract of employment. Therefore, for example, a company might have a retirement age of 60 for both men and women. However, for most companies the question of retirement is related to a pension scheme.

The retirement age that is specified by the employer—the normal retirement age in the undertaking—is the age at which the employee ceases to have the right to complain to an industrial tribunal of unfair dismissal (except for certain specified reasons). The right to a statutory redundancy pay is related to the statutory retirement age.

See Practice Note 3.19.

2.20   Employment of relatives

The Company will consider the employment of relatives of Company employees but this is entirely discretionary on the part of the Company.

The Company reserves the right not to employ relatives together in areas, or relationships, where it considers this undesirable. If existing employees become related the Company may require the relocation of either of the employees and the provisions on relationships will apply.

2.21   Property

Your personal property, including motor cars, money and other valuables, on Company property is there entirely at your own risk. The Company will not accept responsibility for loss or damage of such property.

2.22 Inventions

The Company reserves certain rights to the use of inventions, whether patentable or not, which are made or developed by employees in the course of their employment.

You must therefore refer to your Supervisor before taking steps to use such an invention outside your employment or to patent it.

Variation

It may be that you will require a wider protection for inventions, such as:

All inventions, improvements, discoveries and formulations developed by you, whether alone or jointly with any other person, during the period of your employment with the Company and arising out of or in consequence of such employment shall become the sole property of the Company.

See Practice Note 3.17.

2.23   Vehicles

The provision of a motor car or other vehicle whether or not private use is allowed, is at the discretion of the Company.

Accordingly, where business needs dictate, the Company shall have the right to withdraw that provision or to change the vehicle and to alter the rules as to its use.

Specific rules may apply to particular vehicles and the user must ascertain before use whether there are such rules and if there are they must be observed (including any relating to private use).

Any employee whose job is in any way dependent upon being able to drive a vehicle must notify the Supervisor immediately if charged with any offence or suffering any disablement which may result in that employee's disqualification from driving.

In circumstances where alternative arrangements are impracticable a disqualification from driving may lead to termination of employment.

See Practice Note 3.20.

2.24 Smoking

Certain areas are designated as no-smoking areas for safety, operational or social reasons. It is strictly forbidden to smoke in such a designated area.

See Practice Note 3.21.

2.25 Discrimination

The Company is unreservedly opposed to any form of discrimination being practised against its employees because of their sex or marital status or on the grounds of race, colour, creed or ethnic or national origin.

The Company is also equally opposed to discrimination on the grounds of membership or non-membership of a trade union.

The Company's policy therefore requires entry to its employment, and progression within it, to be based upon merit.

If you feel that you have been discriminated against on any of these grounds you should complain to the Personnel Manager and a full investigation will be made.

Variations

Although there are no special provisions in the employment protection legislation relating to physical disability it can be properly argued that to discriminate on this ground may be unfair in general terms. You may therefore wish to include the following statement:

Physical handicap or disability is of itself no bar to recruitment or advancement within the Company. The main criterion being the ability to perform the job.

You may also wish to include:

Discrimination on any of the above grounds will incur disciplinary action.

See Practice Note 3.22.

2.26 Personal problems

The Company will always endeavour to help employees who may have personal problems or worries, whether connected with work or not. Your Supervisor or Head of Department will listen in confidence to your problem and will, with the resources of the Company, contact any external person or organisation capable of being of assistance to you whenever practicable.

2.27 Personnel records

The Personnel Department maintains a personal file for each employee. The file contains a copy of your statement of terms and conditions of employment. It also contains all other personal documentation such as: salary, benefits, appraisal, medical, engagement, disciplinary records and general correspondence. Access to these records is strictly controlled by the Head of Personnel. Records are also kept of employees who have left the Company's employment.

The Personnel Department will keep these records up-to-date. However, it is your responsibility to inform the Personnel Department at once of all relevant changes, particularly: name, home address, telephone numbers, personal bank details, next of kin, marital status, family status, pension or life insurance benefit nominations, emergency contact information, qualifications including examination results.

All employees will be entitled to view the contents of their own files held by the Personnel Department, with the following exceptions:

- Medical reports.
- References or other correspondence given to the Company in confidence.
- Confidential reports, other than appraisal forms, of a predictive nature, e.g. potential for promotion.

An employee who wants access to his file must make a request through the Head of Department. Examination will then be allowed in the presence of the Head of Department or other appropriate Personnel Officer.

2.28   Personal finance and loans

If you experience personal financial difficulties you may consult your Head of Department or the Personnel Department. It may be that the Company will be able to be of help to you.

Application may be made for an interest-free loan for the purchase of a season ticket for travel by the applicant only between the Company and the home of the employee.

Application may be made for a personal loan for the purchase of goods such as motor cars, household equipment and so on.

The granting of any of the above benefits is at the sole discretion of the Company.

Repayment of any loans shall be at the rate and frequency and in the form notified by the Company. The employee will be provided with a copy of the relevant conditions on application.

Variation

Loans to employees are not available except in the most exceptional circumstances involving personal hardship which cannot be resolved in any other way. Any such exceptional loan that is made is entirely at the discretion of, and on the terms specified by, the Company. Under no circumstances will loans be given for the purchase of consumer products or motor cars.

2.29   Telephone calls

Employees are not allowed to make personal telephone calls except in an emergency or for urgent personal needs. Any such calls that are not local must be reported to the Head of Department. Prior permission must be obtained for personal overseas calls.

2.30   Notice boards

Notice boards are displayed at .... It is important that you read the notices displayed thereon. Only authorised persons are allowed to display notices.

2.31   Collections

Any employee who wishes to take a cash collection for any purpose including, for example, weddings and birthdays, must first obtain permission from the Head of the Department in which it is proposed to collect.

2.32   Suggestion scheme

The Company encourages all employees to make suggestions to improve systems, working practices, customer service or the development of new products.
You should submit any original scheme that you may have, in writing, to
....
A cash award will be made to an employee whose suggestion is accepted.

2.33   Security

All employees are reminded of the constant need to maintain a high level of security.

Staff identity (ID) cards
All employees are issued with an ID card. These cards are labelled with an expiry date and will be renewed as appropriate. Cards must be carried at all times when you are on the Company's premises and must be shown upon request by the security staff or management. Periodic checks may be carried out.

If you change your name or appearance or lose your ID card you must notify your Head of Department immediately.

On leaving the Company's employ your ID card must be returned to your Head of Department.

Visitors
Visitors on the Company's premises must be accompanied by an employee at all times. If you see any person on the premises who arouses your suspicions you should notify your Head of Department immediately.

Equipment and documents
You must take care that if you are absent from your office either temporarily or overnight that all removable equipment, such as small calculators, all confidential documents and all monies and other valuable articles are locked away.

Shredding machines must be used for destroying confidential papers; they must not be deposited in waste bins.

When travelling on public transport, special care must be taken to ensure that confidential papers are not overseen by other travellers.

Searches
Employees on the Company's premises may be subject to security examination of any vehicle or baggage or other possession which is their property or of which they have charge.

Any employee subject to search may require the presence of any other available fellow employee during the search.

For the avoidance of doubt, it is emphasised that this does not include a body search.

See Practice Note 3.23.

2.34   Health and safety at work

The Company is concerned for the health, safety and welfare of all its employees, so far as is reasonably practicable, under the terms of the Health and Safety at Work Act. In order to comply with the provisions of the Act, the Company's health and safety policy is as follows:

- to provide and maintain a safe and healthy working environment for all its employees, customers and others legitimately using the Company's premises.
- To ensure that all employees receive adequate information, instruction and training for the evacuation of the Company's premises in the event of fire or other emergency.
- To investigate any accident occurring on the Company's premises, analyse its cause and take any corrective action.
- To provide all employees with the necessary information, instruction, training and supervision to work safely and efficiently.
- To ensure that, as far as is reasonably practicable, any plant, machinery or equipment provided for use is safe in its operation.
- To ensure that adequate first-aid facilities are available within the Company.
- To ensure that all employees are aware of their legal and moral obligations to take reasonable care for the health and safety of themselves and others, by observing all safety regulations and promptly reporting any potential hazards to the Company Safety Officer.

Every Head of Department, and in his absence appointed deputy, has a day-to-day responsibility to ensure safe and healthy working conditions in his own area, and ensuring that employees are familiar with Company policy in respect of safety, fire precautions and first aid. Work routines should be regularly reviewed to ensure that only the safest work practices, use of machines, etc. are followed.

A copy of the 1974 Health and Safety at Work Act can be obtained from the Personnel Department.

Variation

This is a generalised model which may suit many businesses.

Some businesses may have special problems and needs which should be covered in a policy. It is impossible for a model to provide for such a wide range of circumstances.

In any case, all but the smallest of businesses, should seek expert advice in identifying and providing for their particular needs.

See Practice Note 3.24.

2.35   First-aid facilities

The names of first aiders are posted on the notice boards. Any employee requiring attention should contact the appointed first aider for that area. Where necessary, an employee requiring treatment should be taken to the sick room located .... It is the first aider's responsibility to assess the situation and decide the correct course of action.

First-aid boxes are located .... and may only normally be opened by qualified first aiders. First aiders are not permitted to dispense pharmaceutical products, including aspirins and related products. In cases of serious illness or injury where there are no first aiders in the Company, the person assisting should dial (9)999 and telephone for an ambulance if deemed necessary. The Head of Department should be kept notified.

Reporting of accidents

You are reminded that any accident, however slight, sustained on the Company's premises must be reported without delay to the Company Safety Officer so that details may be entered in the accident book. This is also important in that it enables corrective action to be taken, where appropriate, to prevent such an occurrence happening again.

Safety awareness

All employees are expected to adopt a safety conscious attitude and be aware of the circumstances which can cause accidents. You should, therefore, report immediately any hazards or potential hazards in your workplace to the Company Safety Officer.

All electrical equipment which does not require continuous operation should be switched off when not in use, and disconnected from the main electricity supply at the end of the day. On no account should you carry out any adjustments to electrical equipment. In the event of a fault developing, the equipment should be switched off and the Supervisor notified of the details.

You should endeavour to keep your workplace in a tidy state at all times. Care should be taken to ensure that cupboard doors and desk drawers are not left open unnecessarily. Only one filing cabinet drawer at a time should be opened to prevent overturning.

Special care should be taken to ensure that rights of way and escape routes are never obstructed. When using machines or tools you must always follow the manufacturer's instructions and never take short-cuts to save time as this can lead to accidents.

As serious injury, especially to the back, can result from improper lifting of equipment, employees should familiarise themselves with the correct method of lifting heavy objects.

2.36 Fire and emergency evacuation procedure

You should carefully read below the procedure to be followed in the event of a fire or other emergency and acquaint yourself with all means of exit from the building.

A notice of the Company's Fire Stewards and deputies for each area is posted on the notice boards and you should take particular note of those Fire Stewards responsible for your area.

If you discover a fire you should immediately notify a Fire Steward or if one is not immediately available you should:

- immediately dial 999 and inform the fire brigade of the details, and
- activate the fire alarm by breaking the glass on the nearest alarm. You should familiarise yourself with the locations of these alarms.

On hearing the alarm warning all employees must leave the building using staircases where appropriate. ON NO ACCOUNT MUST THE LIFTS BE USED.

In a fire evacuation it is the Fire Steward's responsibility to ensure that no employee, customer or visitor is left behind and to check that doors and windows have been closed.

Whilst safety to the individual is of paramount importance, you should endeavour to protect any Company records under your control, if time permits, either by placing them in fire-resistant cabinets or removing them to safety as far as is reasonably practicable.

On evacuating the premises you should assemble in the places designated on the notice boards and form departmental groups so that a roll-call can ensure that nobody is left in the building.

On no account should any employee re-enter the building until the fire brigade declare it safe to do so.

If it should happen that a Fire Steward is not available at an emergency the senior staff member in the area should take control.

Fire alarms are normally audible throughout the building, and to familiarise employees with the sound of the alarms and evacuation procedures, testing of the alarms and fire drill will be carried out from time to time, and you are required to co-operate fully.

If a fire of a minor nature is discovered, for example a smouldering waste bin, you should use common sense in extinguishing it. AT NO TIME SHOULD YOU TAKE ANY PERSONAL RISK.

You must familiarise yourself with the locations of fire extinguishers which must not be removed from their positions except for use in emergency. It is important that you understand which extinguishers may or may not be used on electrical fires.

Any use of or accidental discharge of fire extinguishers must be reported to a Fire Steward immediately.

The risk of damage and suffering from fires or other disasters can be minimised if the following points are observed:

- Keep all fire exit doors, fire extinguishers and hose-reel cupboards clear of obstruction at all times.
- Do not block corridors with boxes of stationery, furniture or equipment.
- Fire doors must be kept closed at all times and not propped open.
- Do not smoke in non-smoking areas.
- Use ashtrays only to extinguish cigarettes, cigars or pipes.
- Report immediately any faulty electrical appliances or fittings.

In the event of fire you should observe these points:

- Lifts must not be used.
- Close BUT DO NOT LOCK all doors and windows if time permits on evacuation to inhibit the spread of fire.
- Do not remain near the scene of the fire.
- Do not waste time in collecting personal belongings.

Report immediately any suspicious parcels or packages BUT DO NOT ATTEMPT TO INVESTIGATE THEM YOURSELF. If it is reasonable to suspect a bomb hazard the above procedure for fires should be carried out but notify the Fire Steward, and where appropriate the fire brigade, of your suspicions.

2.37 Training and education

Policy statement

The Company views training as making an important contribution to its efficiency and profitability, and specifically aims to:

- Encourage employees to attend relevant external training courses, seminars and courses of study which will develop their knowledge.
- Improve the capabilities of employees thereby enhancing their abilities to attain the highest possible standards in their jobs.
- Realise the potential of employees by developing and preparing them for increased responsibility and promotion.
- Enable the Company to ensure employees are adequately trained to meet the challenge resulting from technological change.

Course nomination procedures

The decision to send an employee on an external training course is based upon the needs of the employee and his job. It is the employee's Supervisor or Head of Department who is responsible for identifying individual training needs, and for consequently nominating employees to be sent on training courses.

Nominations for all courses are to be approved by the Head of Department.

Employees attending training courses will be paid at the normal hourly rate. Any expenses that are necessary to attendance at the course, including any travel expenses, will be reimbursed on presentation to the Company of proof of expenditure.

Examination fees

The Company will reimburse employees for the cost of their fees for examinations taken at a first sitting.

Tuition fees and textbooks

The Company will refund employees half the cost of the tuition fees, and pay half the cost of textbooks designated as essential reading, subject to the following maximum amounts:

	Maximum	
Stage	Tuition fees	Text books
	£ ...	£ ...

The Company may make discretionary awards to employees passing other examinations such as Open University examinations recognised by the Company as being relevant.

The employee concerned should notify .... at once of the examination results and forward a copy of any certificates obtained.

The granting of an award itself does not have any salary or promotion relevance, but simply aims to recognise effort and achievement.

Professional memberships

The Company will pay the annual subscription fee to the professional body to which you belong, where management considers that membership is relevant to the performance of your job. Membership fees should be submitted to

....

Study leave

If it should be that a particular course of training would be enhanced by a period of concentrated study, the Company will give consideration to a period of study-leave. Any such leave that is allowed will be on terms, set down in writing by the Company, as to duration, salary, cost and expenses.

In-situ training

Where an employee is required to undergo in-situ job training, for a period of induction to the Company or on a change of job or on an introduction of new practices or technology, the rate of payment and other terms shall be as laid down in a Trial Training Agreement or Trial Training Requirement, as appropriate.

2.38   Redundancy policy

It is the intention of the Company, as far as is possible, to maintain full employment. However, good industrial relations require that we state Company policy in case redundancy ever becomes necessary.

If it appears that there is to be a diminution or cessation of work that is likely to be of a short-term duration management will examine the practicability of introducing a period of lay-off or short-time working.

Where redundancy appears to be necessary, management will examine the possibility of job changes in accordance with the Alternative Employment provisions of these rules.

Where termination of employment by reason of redundancy appears to be inevitable, management will notify employees concerned of the categories to be affected and any queries about those categories must be raised with management immediately.

Should any selection within those categories be necessary management will decide it on the basis of retaining those who, in the opinion of management after due consideration, are likely to contribute most to the future prosperity of the Company and therefore the job security of all, including such factors as length of service, absenteeism and written warnings. Any queries about selection must be raised with management immediately.

During the redundancy consultation period management will take into consideration any representations or suggestions for inclusion in or alteration to this policy.

Any employee who has a grievance relating to redundancy must raise that grievance immediately with the Head of Department and the grievance will be heard in accordance with the Hearings provisions of these rules.

Variations

If you have elected not to have a lay-off or short-time provision in your contract then you cannot unilaterally impose lay-off or short-time working. Therefore, you may wish to delete the second paragraph of the model clause or to amend it as follows:

If it appears that there is to be a diminution or cessation of work that is likely to be of a short-term duration, management will examine the practicability of offering to the affected employees a period of lay-off or short-time working.

Redundancy procedures cannot be introduced or changed at whim. If the Company has an agreed redundancy procedure, or one which has become customary, that procedure must continue to be followed unless it can be shown that there is some overriding need to change. Therefore, it may be that some companies will have different methods of selection for redundancy. For example, it may be that the first sentence of the fifth paragraph of the model clause will need to be altered, e.g.:

> Should any selection within those categories be necessary management will decide it on the basis of selecting those who have the shortest periods of continuous employment.

The last sentence of that paragraph should be retained.

A selection policy may also include voluntary redundancy. However, care needs to be taken in this regard where it is possible that the number of volunteers may fall short of or exceed the number required:

> Before the process of selection is commenced the Company will invite employees within the specified categories to volunteer for redundancy. (For the avoidance of doubt, no employee outside the specified category will be accepted as a volunteer.) If it should happen that the number of volunteers falls short of the required number, the balance required will be selected as above. If it should happen that the number of volunteers exceeds the required number the above selection method will be applied to the volunteers only and to no other employee.

See Practice Note 3.25.

2.39   Grievance procedure

The appeals procedure relating to discipline or dismissal is provided for in the Appeals provisions of these rules.

Any grievance that you might have relating to your employment (for example about pay, your work, supervision, holidays and so on) should first be taken up with your Supervisor. If that grievance relates to your Supervisor you may go direct to your Head of Department.

Failing settlement at that stage if you wish to pursue the matter further you must put the matter in writing to your Head of Department for it to be referred to more senior management.

Your grievance will then be dealt with as soon as is reasonably practicable and you will be notified of the result immediately thereafter.

See Practice Note 3.26.

2.40   Notice

The notice you have to give to terminate your employment is one calendar month unless more is required in the particular case by an attached addendum.

The notice you are entitled to receive to terminate your employment is one calendar month increasing after four years of employment by one week for each succeeding full year of employment up to a maximum of twelve weeks' notice except where otherwise provided for in an attached addendum.

The Company may require you to take paid leave of absence during all or any part of a period of notice.

Variations

You may wish to include:

The Company may give pay in lieu of notice.

However, it should be noted that if this provision is included the act of giving pay in lieu of notice will thereby not be a breach of contract. Consequently, it will not be a payment of damages and you may be required by the Authorities to treat the lieu pay as wages for the purpose of statutory deductions.

It is also arguable that such a provision is contrary to the requirement of law that an agreement to take away a statutory right is invalid. The statutory notice requirement is:

The notice you are required to give to terminate your employment is one week after one month of employment.

The notice you are entitled to receive to terminate your employment is one week after one month of employment, two weeks after two years of employment and an additional one week of notice for each additional complete year of employment up to a maximum of twelve weeks of notice.

See Practice Note 3.27.

2.41   Gross misconduct

In cases which management believes to be gross misconduct the employee will be suspended from work pending a hearing.

Where, following that hearing, management is satisfied that dismissal is appropriate it will be immediate and without notice. It may be without notice pay and the period of suspension will not be paid.

Where management decides that dismissal is not appropriate, but that disciplinary action is justified, it may substitute a warning and the period of suspension may be paid or not as management deems appropriate. In addition, a further period of suspension may be imposed which shall not exceed five working days and which shall be unpaid.

Where management decides that disciplinary action was inappropriate the period of suspension will be paid and the action expunged from the employee's records.

Variations

If you decide not to include a list of examples of misconduct you may wish to include the following:

These Rules do not include examples of gross misconduct. The Company will treat each case of misconduct on its merits and, where a particular act is regarded as being fundamental to the operation of the Company or its industrial relations, it will be treated as gross misconduct.

In cases which management believes to be gross misconduct the employee will be suspended from work pending a hearing.

Where, following that hearing, management is satisfied that dismissal is appropriate it will be immediate and without notice. It may be without notice pay and the period of suspension will not be paid.

Where management decides that dismissal is not appropriate, but that disciplinary action is justified, it may substitute a warning and the period of suspension may be paid or not as management deems appropriate. In addition, a further period of suspension may be imposed which shall not exceed five working days and which shall be unpaid.

Where management decides that disciplinary action was inappropriate the period of suspension will be paid and the action expunged from the employee's records.

See Practice Note 3.28.

2.42   Warnings

Written warnings are permanently kept on file, as are records of oral warnings. These may be taken into account when determining such matters as promotion, pay, benefits, redundancy selection and so on.

However, no warning will be activated for the purpose of disciplinary proceedings after a period of six months following the date of the issue of the warning except, where that warning relates to a period specified in excess of six months. For example, when a warning is given relating to late return to work after holidays.

See Practice Note 3.29.

2.43   Misconduct examples

Where an act of misconduct is regarded by management as so fundamental to the operation of the Company or its industrial relations that it would be inappropriate to give a warning prior to consideration of dismissal it will be treated as gross misconduct above.

Examples which, when these issues affect the Company, will normally be regarded as gross misconduct are as follows:

- Unauthorised disclosure of Company information.
- Behaviour prejudicial to the good name of the Company.
- Gross negligence or insubordination.
- Theft or fraud.
- Violent behaviour.
- Wilful breach of safety regulations, endangering the safety of other persons or equipment.
- Wilful damage to Company property.
- Offensive behaviour or language.
- Drunkenness.
- Dishonesty.
- Drug abuse.
- Betting or gambling on Company property.

These are examples only and this is not an exhaustive list.

See Practice Note 3.28.

2.44   Cautionary matters

In cases of misconduct, which are considered by management not to be gross misconduct, or inadequate work-performance or any other matter requiring cautionary measures, the employee may be told orally of the matter of complaint.

In the event of any further occurrence or failure to correct the matter of complaint, or on a serious first occurrence, a final warning of dismissal will be given.

In a case of further complaint by management the employee will be suspended from work pending a hearing.

Where, following that hearing, management is satisfied that dismissal is appropriate it will be with notice and the period of suspension may be paid or not as management deems appropriate.

If management decides that dismissal is not appropriate it may substitute a further warning and the period of suspension may be paid or not as management deems appropriate.

When management decides that the disciplinary action was inappropriate the period of suspension will be paid and the action expunged from the employee's records.

See Practice Note 3.28.

Sickness and injury cautions

Unauthorised absence from work or absence that is unsupported by a sickness certificate will be treated as misconduct.

Management may require any employee to undergo at any reasonable time a medical examination by a doctor appointed by the Company. Failure to comply will render it necessary for management to take a decision based upon its own view of the employee's condition.

Management will take account of any report submitted from the employee's own doctor but if that conflicts with the report from the Company's doctor the latter will normally be regarded as the more persuasive.

In cases where the management believes that an employee is unable to continue work to a satisfactory standard because of a health condition the problem will be discussed with the employee and, where the condition allows, a hearing will be convened. There will be no period of suspension but, where the employee is not on sick leave, any reasonable time off will be allowed, on request, for the employee to prepare for the hearing.

If, following enquiries, management believes that it is appropriate that the employment should be terminated it will be with notice.

The time off provided for in this section will be paid.

Variations

Some authorities believe that it is safer, if the company doctor and the employee's doctor disagree, to put the question to a third doctor, preferably a specialist. If you wish to do that the third paragraph of the model would need alteration as below:

Unauthorised absence from work or absence that is unsupported by a sickness certificate will be treated as misconduct.

Management may require any employee to undergo at any reasonable time a medical examination by a doctor appointed by the Company, whether or not there has been a recent record of sickness. Failure to comply will render it necessary for management to take a decision based upon its own view of the employee's condition.

Management will take account of any report submitted from the employee's own doctor but if that conflicts with the report from the Company's doctor the Company will arrange for the employee to be examined by a third doctor, where possible a specialist recommended by the Company's doctor. The report from that doctor shall be the conclusive report unless that doctor recommends otherwise.

In cases where the management believes that an employee is unable to continue work to a satisfactory standard because of a health condition the problem will be discussed with the employee and, where the condition allows, a hearing will be convened. There will be no period of suspension but, where the employee is not on sick leave, any reasonable time off will be allowed, on request, for the employee to prepare for the hearing.

If, following enquiries, management believes that it is appropriate that the employment should be terminated it will be with notice.

The time off provided for in this section will be paid.

See Practice Note 3.30.

2.45   Hearings

Where there is a hearing held in accordance with these rules the employee shall attend the hearing at a place and at a time designated by management during working hours. In the event of a failure by the employee to do so the hearing shall be held in the employee's absence. However, if immediately following the notification of the decision of management the employee shows good cause for not so attending the decision shall be revoked and a further hearing convened.

The employee shall state his case and management shall hear any person called by them or the employee concerned who has information material to the issue.

The employee concerned may be accompanied by any other fellow employee or be represented by any fellow employee. In cases where there are implications that could lead to criminal prosecution, or where such proceedings are pending, the employee may have present at the hearing a legal adviser whose function shall be only that of ensuring that the employee's position is not prejudiced in relation to such legal proceedings.

Variation

A company which has trade union representation may wish to include:

A trade union representative is required to conform to normal standards of conduct and work-performance and no allowance will be accorded to a representative in this regard. However, representatives shall be entitled to be represented at a hearing by a full-time officer of the appropriate trade union provided such representation does not unduly delay hearing proceedings.

See Practice Note 3.31.

2.46   Suspension

A period of suspension that is preparatory to a hearing shall not normally be for longer than five working days or shorter than one day. Where a hearing is held beyond this period at the instigation of management the extra period will be paid.

See Practice Note 3.32.

2.47   Alternative employment

In appropriate cases where there is a prospect of dismissal relating to matters unconnected with conduct the Company will examine any alternative employment for which there is at that time a suitable vacancy.

Any alternative employment that is offered will be at the rate of pay and conditions relating to the job that is offered.

Variation

In appropriate cases where there is a prospect of dismissal relating to matters unconnected with conduct the Company will examine any alternative employment for which there is at that time a suitable vacancy.

Any alternative employment that is offered will be at the rate of pay and conditions relating to the job that is offered, except that management may, at its discretion, continue the previously held rate of pay for a period of ... months following the change as determined by management to be appropriate.

See Practice Note 3.33.

2.48 Appeals

The Grievance Procedure shall be the process of appeal for matters unconnected with discipline or termination of employment.

Where disciplinary action has been taken against an employee short of dismissal, that employee shall have the right to appeal within five working days.

The appeal shall be put in writing and shall be delivered to the employee's supervisor.

A dismissed person may appeal as stated above within five working days of notification of dismissal in which case the dismissal shall be suspended pending the outcome of the appeal.

Where possible an appeal shall be conducted by members of management not involved in any earlier disciplinary action or hearings with which the appeal is concerned and the provisions in the hearings section shall apply.

There shall be no suspension or time-off allowance prior to an appeal hearing but where employment has ceased the period up to the appeal will be paid if the appeal is upheld but not otherwise.

See Practice Note 3.34.

Part Three
Practice Notes

Contents of Part Three

Note: These practice notes are intended to explain the requirements of the legislation or to show the reasons for the inclusion of, or the wording of, a particular rule. Therefore, not all rules will have a related practice note but where they do the appropriate reference is given at the end of each section.

3.1   Statement of terms

The law requires that an employer must give to every new employee, within 13 weeks of engagement, a statement of the main terms and conditions of employment.

The model statement (see Contract Documentation 1.1) contains all of the information that is specified by law.

The legislation allows for that statement to refer to other documents where the information can be seen. Therefore, this model makes use of that provision by referring extensively to an employment rules book. This has the advantage that standard terms can be devised which can be easily read and understood and avoids the necessity of reissuing statements if a rule has to be changed.

Some employees may have conditions which will be different from those standardised in the rule book. In that case the statement can be used to particularise those differences.

The statement of terms given in accordance with the law is not in itself a contract of employment. It is merely a statement of opinion by the employer as to what, in the employer's view, certain parts of the contract are.

Where that statement, and any referred rules, are given to a new employee there will be a presumption in law that the new employee has consented to those terms and conditions by accepting the job. Therefore, that statement will be powerful evidence that the employee is bound by the terms of the statement and rules.

However, if changes are made later on to which the employee does not expressly agree, there will be no presumption that the employee is bound by the changes. Therefore, it is important, wherever possible, when a change is made to obtain from the employee a signed statement of acceptance. The employer may well have to offer some inducement to gain that acceptance—perhaps an improvement in some benefit.

If the employer has some overwhelming business need to make a change it may be that it can be introduced whether or not the employee consents. However, this calls for some measure of subjective judgement on the importance of the change.

If a change is made, the statement or the rule book must be amended within one month.

See Contract Documentation 1.1.

3.2   Contract of employment

A contract of employment, as distinct from a statement of terms, is a contract between the employer and the employee binding both parties to the terms expressed in the contract.

There is little practical difference between a contract and a statement. The latter can be as binding as the former provided it is properly devised, and provided changes are expressly accepted by the employee (where necessary).

Whatever documentation is used to record the terms and conditions of employment the rules regarding changes are the same, as set out in Practice Note 3.1.

It may be that there will be other documents which should be referred to in the statement such as a pension fund booklet.

However, it is important that it is understood that whether a statement of terms is used or a more formal contract, there may be factors or practices outside the written documentation which will also be contractually binding upon the parties. Thus, if payments are made which are not set out in the documentation it may well be that they will be said to be part of the contract of employment.

It is useful, therefore, to regard a contract of employment as being the whole of the relationship between employer and employee, with the documentation recording all of the more important parts of that relationship.

Should it happen that some term or practice changes from that which is recorded in the documentation it could be held that any change to the advantage of the employee has become contractually binding, but that any unagreed change can be repudiated by the employee.

It is therefore important that the documentation be periodically reviewed to see that it accords with current practice.

It is also useful to check that documentation accords with current legal requirements.

Fairness, as defined by law, is dependent upon the employer keeping abreast of current good practice and documentation and procedures should be reviewed in this light from time to time.

A contract of service (employment contract) entitles the employee to all employee rights as specified by the employment protection legislation.

A contract for services is where a person's services are used in a sub-contractor-like fashion. Such as where a person is commissioned to carry out some sort of one-off assignment. That status does not carry with it employment protection rights except in the field of race or sex discrimination.

See Contract Documentation 1.2 and 1.3.

3.3 Agreement for services

The term "agreement of service" is applied to a contract of employment. Under that type of agreement the parties are subject to normal employment law.

An agreement for services is for a person or company to provide a commercial service. That is, the parties have a temporary contractual relationship for a specific purpose and are not subject to the mainstream of employment law.

Such an agreement is useful when work has to be carried out where employees would not normally be available. Perhaps consultancy assignments where a consultant will work within an organisation to achieve a specific objective within a limited period.

Clearly, one cannot use agreements for services to avoid the problems of employment law.

The dividing line between an employment contract and a non-employment contract can often be difficult to discern. On the one hand if a contractor is hired, perhaps to install equipment, that will clearly be a contract for services. On the other hand, if a single individual is hired to carry out some function that would normally be undertaken by an employee, the mere fact that the parties may have entered into a contract for service may not be sufficient to indicate a non-employment contract.

The fact that the worker has an arrangement with the Authorities so that income tax and national insurance is not deducted may be evidence of a non-employment relationship, but it is not necessarily conclusive evidence.

If the point comes to be tested in law, a major factor will be the degree of control that can be exercised over the worker. In short, if the worker is treated like an employee in the way that work is allocated and control is exercised, that may be taken as proof of employment.

It is therefore a matter of judgement for the parties as to whether engagement should be by way of a contract for services or whether an employment contract is more appropriate.

If the work is to be carried out can be specified in terms of time, a fixed-term contract of employment may be more appropriate than either a contract for services or an open-ended employment contract.

Even when it is certain beyond doubt that a person who carries out work for a company is not an employee, that person will still have rights under the race relations, sex discrimination and equal pay legislation.

The model supplied here would be useful where the worker cannot be said to be an employee.

See Contract Documentation 1.4.

3.4 Foreword

A foreword can have a number of uses, for example, as in the model, it can:

- draw to the attention of the employee, and to members of an industrial tribunal if needs be, that standards of behaviour and work are not just vague concepts and that poor standards may have an effect on other employees;
- remove any excuse that an employee may make, claiming that he did not know of a rule because of lost copy;
- deal with how amendments will be notified;
- provide definitions.

The foreword should be restricted to dealing with rules-related matters and should not be complicated with irrelevant information. If it is desired to say something about the history of the company, or to describe its structure, it is better to include it elsewhere, perhaps in a separate booklet or leaflet.

See Employment Rules Book 2.1.

3.5   Hours of work

It is a requirement of the legislation that if an employee is required to work normal hours then those hours must be notified to that employee by way of the statement of terms of particulars of employment, or a referred document such as a rules book.

It is useful, for the sake of clarity, to state the starting and finishing times, including breaks, and the total 'normal hours' for the week. Normal hours are the hours that the employee must work under the contract of employment. Therefore, the position regarding overtime also needs to be clarified, even when overtime is never required—in which case this should be stated.

Of course, if overtime is ever likely then the pay for overtime hours also needs to be made clear. For example, whether overtime is to be paid at plain time rates or premium rates; and if at premium rates, what those rates are.

Some companies may wish to set a ceiling on overtime rates, e.g. £x maximum hourly rate. Another method is to set overtime rates against salary bands; for example, employees in the band £z000 to £y000 would be paid overtime at the rate of £x an hour.

If overtime hours are always voluntary then they will not count for the purpose of calculating such statutory entitlements as redundancy pay. However, if overtime is compulsory then it will count, and it may well be that the employee would have a right to work those compulsory hours.

It is sometimes impossible to define normal hours—this is often so for executives. However, the position still needs clarification, perhaps by the statement that the hours required are whatever reasonable hours the needs of the job dictate. In this case it should also be made clear that the salary paid is inclusive of all hours worked, that is that there is no overtime pay.

Many of the legislative employee rights depend upon the employee being a 'full-time' employee, that is someone who is normally employed for 16 or more hours weekly. However, if that person has been in that employment for five years or more the full-time benefits apply to normal hours of eight or more weekly.

Furthermore, if an employee's hours are reduced to below 16 but to more than eight a week that employee retains full-time status for the ensuing 26 weeks, notwithstanding that the period of continuous employment is less than five years.

As with any other part of the contract of employment, hours of work are normally only changeable by mutual agreement.

See Employment Rules Book 2.2.

3.6   Holidays

Holiday entitlement can be a source of grievance for employees and so it is important that holiday allowance and conditions of entitlement are stipulated very clearly.

There are no statutory provisions covering holiday entitlement (except for those industries subject to Wage Council Regulations) and the conditions which attach to entitlement need to be established by the individual employer.

The model contained in 2.3 of the Rules Book covers the most important points.

See Employment Rules Book 2.3.

3.7   Probation

There is no special provision in law for probationary periods. An employer may specify for new employees any reasonable period. Or, indeed, not mention any period at all.

There are two main uses for probationary periods. The first is to emphasise to the new employee that certain standards have to be met and that dismissal will result from failure to maintain those standards throughout the period. (The counter-argument to this is that the employee may be inspired to set a standard for the period of probation which cannot be sustained long term.) The second is to have a period which has to be completed before specified benefits commence, such as entry to the pension scheme.

The law itself provides what may be called a 'probationary period'. That is the period which qualifies for rights under the law. Examples are: one month before the statutory right to notice commences; two years before the right not to be unfairly dismissed accrues and so on. (See Part Five, the Law Check.)

Therefore, although the employer is free to set whatever probationary period is reasonable, that cannot take away from the employee any of the rights provided by statute.

It follows that if a probationary period is longer than that allowed by law for claiming unfair dismissal, the employee cannot be denied that statutory right by the rule on probation.

Similarly, if the period is shorter than that provided by law for claiming unfair dismissal the employee will not acquire the right to so claim until the statutory period is completed.

Common law rights will, of course, subsist from the moment the contract of employment commences.

See Employment Rules Book 2.4.

3.8   Remuneration

The contract of employment is a mutual agreement between parties whereby the employee undertakes to perform duties, and to observe rules in exchange for pay and perhaps other benefits. Therefore, any part of the contract which deals with pay or benefits needs to be very clear as to the entitlement.

Apart from some small businesses which are subject to Wage Council Regulations, employers are free to offer whatever pay they think reasonable and to update pay levels at intervals and at rates as they desire. Legislation does not interfere with pay determination (except for the laws on equality). It may be that in some employments pay increases have to be negotiated with recognised trade unions or are set by joint industry-wide bodies.

Of course, if the contract of employment requires pay reviews or even stipulates pay rises then such terms have to be observed.

The only recourse to industrial tribunals an employee has with regard to pay is where there is a disagreement as to whether the employer is actually carrying out a term of contract on pay that already exists in the contract. In that case the employee, or even the employer for that matter, can ask a tribunal for a ruling; the tribunal cannot make any financial award, its powers are limited to making a declaration as to whether there is an existing liability in terms of the statutory right to be notified about pay. Any such finding would very likely be enforceable through other courts.

It is a term of every contract of employment, whether actually written down or not, that there shall be no discrimination between men and women with regard to remuneration. Any person, man or woman, who does feel that there is such inequality is able to appeal to an industrial tribunal for redress; in this case, of course, tribunals are empowered to make financial awards as well as declarations.

Equality may be determined by direct job comparison or by comparing the value of jobs.

These rights which relate to sex discrimination extend beyond direct employees. Thus, if a company uses contract workers or even self-employed persons, they will also be covered.

There is an increasing use in industry of evaluation schemes which are relied upon to determine wage levels. If such a scheme is adopted its rules and mechanisms should be explained to employees and need to be demonstrably fair.

See Employment Rules Book 2.5.

3.9   Job title

The legislation requires that when an employee is engaged the employer must define the job title. This has to be done by way of the statement of particulars of employment that is given in writing to employees within 13 weeks of engagement.

There is nothing in the legislation that requires the employer to define the job by way of a job description, merely the provision of a job title. For the majority of jobs this is sufficient. There may be cases where it is felt that a job description would be more beneficial, but if that is the case great care should be taken in its formulation. Job descriptions can be restrictive and as such are best left to specialists.

A job title should be precise enough to convey to the employee, and others, a reasonable understanding of the broad scope of duties it covers without breaking down those duties into detailed items of work. On the other hand a job title should not be so broad that it is meaningless. For example, the description 'clerk' does not necessarily give the employer freedom to move a clerk around at will. Some clerks will have specialised in particular types of work and, if that is the case, the job title should reflect that specialisation. For example, the title 'shorthand typist' will tell the employee exactly what the broad outline of duties are. Thus, with an appropriate transfer clause, an employee with that job title would be expected to undertake any shorthand typing work within the geographical area defined in the job location part of the contract of employment.

It is therefore advisable to add to the job title a note requiring that the employee must be available for duties somewhat outside that job title (see the Rules Book 2.7) so that the employee cannot use the job title to set restrictive parameters to the job. Of course, clauses which do widen the scope of a job title can only do so within the bounds of reasonability and within the bounds of the employee's capability. Such clauses cannot be used to alter permanently the work which the employee is engaged to do. Such a clause must be used sparingly, when necessity dictates and for the purpose of overcoming temporary difficulties.

A complete change to the job title where the nature of the work the employee is employed to do alters can only normally be achieved with the consent of the employee. In some cases it may be that some inducement will be necessary to achieve the desired result.

However, there may be circumstances where a change is unavoidable; where, for example, reorganisation dictates a change and where the only alternative would be to make the employee redundant. In such circumstances, where the job will no longer exist, there is an obligation on the employer to try to offer suitable alternative employment. (See the redundancy practice note, section 3.25.)

See Employment Rules Book 2.7.

3.10 Place of employment

A transfer clause whereby an employee can be moved from one job location to another must be reasonable and it must reflect the realities of the nature of the undertaking.

There are two sorts of transfer: that which allows a move within an establishment; and that which allows a transfer to a completely different location (perhaps to a different part of the country, or even abroad).

It may make sense to require that, say, a shorthand typist be transferred from one office to another within the same building provided there are discernible and good reasons for so doing. However, it may be unreasonable, whatever the contract of employment says, to require such a shorthand typist to move to a different location many miles away.

On the other hand there may well be certain types of employee, particularly managers, whose work necessitates changes of location from time to time. If that is so, then that requirement should be written into the contract of employment, and not left to implication or custom and practice.

When a transfer clause is contained in a contract of employment, and where it is clearly applicable, such a transfer is a requirement of a contract. It does not of itself change the contract.

Obviously, if there is some other change that occurs at the same time as the transfer, such as a change in duties that is not provided for in the contract, then that change would normally be negotiable with the employee.

The contract of employment should also make clear any other matters that are consequent upon a transfer; that is, relocation costs, the loss of any city weighting allowances and so on.

See Employment Rules Book 2.8.

3.11 Maternity

Statutory Maternity Pay (SMP) is payable by the employer for a maximum of 18 weeks and this period is called the Maternity Pay Period (MPP). The employee must give her employer at least 21 days' notice (in writing if so required) that she will be absent from work due to pregnancy or confinement to be eligible for SMP.

Three main conditions must be fulfilled by the employee if she is to qualify for SMP.

(i)   She must have at least 26 weeks or two years (working 16 hours a week or more) or five years (working between eight and 16 hours a week) continuous service up to and including at least one day in the Qualifying Week (QW). (The QW (Sunday to Saturday) is the 15th week before the Expected Week of Confinement (EWC).)

(ii)   Her average weekly earnings in the eight weeks prior to the QW must be not less than the current lower earnings limit for class one national insurance contributions.

(iii) She must have reached the beginning of the eleventh week before the EWC or must have given birth to a live baby before that date although she can stop work at the start of the fourteenth week before her EWC. (The EWC is the week in which the baby is due to be born as certified ideally on a Form MAT B1 (maternity certificate).)

SMP is paid at one of two rates. The higher rate for the first six weeks of the MPP is nine tenths of the woman's average weekly earnings, and is payable to her if she has been continuously employed for at least two years immediately preceding the 14th week before the EWC or for five years continuous service for a woman who normally works between eight and 16 hours per week. The lower rate of SMP is payable for a maximum of 12 weeks if the woman has been paid the higher rate during the first six weeks or for a maximum of 18 weeks if the woman is not eligible for the higher rate, and to qualify for the lower rate the woman must have been continuously employed for 26 weeks prior to and including at least one day of the QW.

There is no daily rate for SMP – it is only paid for whole weeks. SMP records must be kept by the employer for a minimum of three years after the tax year to which they relate.

Any contractual payments, ie wages, maternity pay or sick pay, are set off against any SMP.

An employee who has been in employment for a continuous period of not less than two years at immediately before the eleventh week before the expected week of her confinement (whether she was actually working or not), is entitled to take time off work because of her pregnancy or confinement.

An employee who takes time off for maternity reasons must inform her employer, in writing, at least 21 days before her absence begins, or as soon as is reasonably practicable, that she will be (or is) absent from work wholly or partly because of pregnancy or confinement and that she intends to return to work.

She can return to her job at any time up to 29 weeks from the week of her confinement. However, if at the end of the 29-week period, or any earlier period she has nominated for return, she is unable to do so because of disease or bodily or mental disablement she can delay her return for up to four weeks. In that case she is required to produce medical evidence for her employer.

The employer can delay her return by up to four weeks from the date she nominates provided she is informed of the reason before the return date.

She is entitled to return to the same job as she previously held and on the same or not less favourable terms and conditions.

If it is not reasonably practicable to permit her to return to the same job the employer can offer her suitable alternative employment which is not substantially less favourable.

The employer may ask the employee at any time after the first 49 days of absence for written confirmation that she still intends to return and, provided the employer has warned her of the consequences, she must reply within 14 days or lose her right to return.

Practice Notes

If the employee cannot notify her return to work because of an interruption to work (such as a strike or lay-off) then she may do so within 14 days of the end of the interruption even if it goes beyond the end of the 29-week period.

If, however, she has nominated her return date and then cannot return because of such an interruption she may return as soon as the interruption ends or as soon thereafter as is reasonably practicable.

See Employment Rules Book 2.9.

Practice Notes

If the employee cannot notify her return to work because of an interruption to work (such as a strike or lay-off) then she may do so within 14 days of the end of the interruption even if it goes beyond the end of the 29-week period.

If, however, she has nominated her return date and then cannot return because of such an interruption she may return as soon as the interruption ends or as soon thereafter as is reasonably practicable.

See Employment Rules Book 2.9.

3.11   Maternity

An employee who has been in employment for a continuous period of not less than two years at immediately before the eleventh week before the expected week of her confinement (whether she was actually working or not), is entitled to take time off work because of her pregnancy or confinement.

She is entitled to be paid for the first six weeks of absence; that is the first six weeks, whether continuous or a broken period, after the beginning of the eleventh week.

A week's pay for this statutory purpose is nine-tenths of normal pay less whatever social security maternity allowance is payable (even if the employee in question is not actually entitled to the whole or any part of that allowance). The employer is entitled to a rebate on this payment claimable from the Maternity Pay Fund.

An employee also has the right to reasonable time off to attend antenatal appointments and to be paid for that time off provided (if the employer requests) she produces (except for the first appointment) a medical certificate or appointment card as proof.

Any contractual pay can be set off against the statutory pay.

An employee who takes time off for maternity reasons must inform her employer, in writing, at least 21 days before her absence begins, or as soon as is reasonably practicable, that she will be (or is) absent from work wholly or partly because of pregnancy or confinement and that she intends to return to work.

She can return to her job at any time up to 29 weeks from the week of her confinement. However, if at the end of the 29-week period, or any earlier period she has nominated for return, she is unable to do so because of disease or bodily or mental disablement she can delay her return for up to four weeks. In that case she is required to produce medical evidence for her employer.

The employer can delay her return by up to four weeks from the date she nominates provided she is informed of the reason before the return date.

She is entitled to return to the same job as she previously held and on the same or not less favourable terms and conditions.

If it is not reasonably practicable to permit her to return to the same job the employer can offer her suitable alternative employment which is not substantially less favourable.

The employer may ask the employee at any time after the first 49 days of absence for written confirmation that she still intends to return and, provided the employer has warned her of the consequences, she must reply within 14 days or lose her right to return.

If the employee cannot notify her return to work because of an interruption to work (such as a strike or lay-off) then she may do so within 14 days of the end of the interruption even if it goes beyond the end of the 29-week period.

If, however, she has nominated her return date and then cannot return because of such an interruption she may return as soon as the interruption ends or as soon thereafter as is reasonably practicable.

See Employment Rules Book 2.9.

3.12   Attendance

Absenteeism can be a costly problem for employers, but there may be occasions when an employee should be allowed time off work for compassionate reasons. It is impossible to list all of these circumstances which may give rise to compassionate leave entitlement, but the question of pay for such absence should be clarified in the rules.

Unauthorised absence needs to be dealt with in the rules. It should be noted that if the rules require that unauthorised absence will be taken into account for certain matters such as promotion, then the records dealing with promoted employees should show that the procedure was enforced – and that applies, of course, to other matters such as redundancy selection.

It is self-evident that all absence from work, for whatever reason, should be carefully recorded. If poor timekeeping is to be a factor considered in promotion then time-clock or other records should be kept (or a periodic summary) for as long as that record is likely to be used.

In some concerns it could be very serious if certain key personnel were prevented from getting to work in an emergency, such as a transport strike or bad weather. For those employers, it would be a sensible precaution to include a similar provision to that stated in the first two sentences of the last paragraph of the Rules Book 2.10.

A wider range of employers could also benefit from the last two sentences of that same paragraph.

See Employment Rules Book 2.10.

3.13   Statutory time off

Those who have statutory time-off rights for public duties are:

- A justice of the peace.
- A member of a local authority.
- A member of a statutory tribunal.
- A member of, in England and Wales, a Regional or Area Health Authority or, in Scotland, a Health Board.
- A member of, in England and Wales, the managing or governing body of an educational establishment maintained by a local education authority or, in Scotland, a school or college council or the governing body of a central institution or a college of education.
- A member of, in England and Wales, a water authority or, in Scotland, a river purification board.

Employees with public duties' responsibilities, as listed, have the statutory right to take whatever time off work is reasonable but they have no statutory right to be paid for that time off.

An employee who feels that such statutory right was denied may apply to an industrial tribunal for redress. If the complaint is upheld by the tribunal it can award compensation to whatever sum it considers to be just and equitable.

See Employment Rules Book 2.11.

3.14   Sickness and injury

This model rule is designed for a company which operates its own sickness certification scheme. See the Variations section for other versions.

Whichever method is adopted, it is advised that management insist that all sickness absence is covered by certification (except where the rules allow an initial day or so without).

Records relating to sickness absence should be kept meticulously, including not only a record of dates of absence but any related documentation such as certificates and medical reports.

It is useful to have a procedure (not necessarily written into the rules) whereby action is initiated in all cases after a stated period of absence, whether a continuous or a broken period. Proceedings for medical examination need not be undertaken at this point, but the position in respect of the employee should be reviewed, and, if no action is taken, kept under review.

If the absence reaches a point where it is felt that something needs to be done then the rules set out in the disciplinary section (p.72) need to be followed.

See Employment Rules Book 2.12.

3.15 Personal appearance

There has been no real guidance from case law about the imposition of standards of dress by employers. Therefore, all that can be said is that employers should adopt a commonsense approach to this problem.

Quite clearly, employers must have some control in dress standards. The test that should be applied is whether a particular mode of dress is likely to have an adverse effect upon the business, not whether it is found to be personally disagreeable. For example, it may well be wrong to bar the wearing of ear-rings by male bricklayers on a building site whilst appropriate to do so in the context of a bank where the employee's position is one where customers could take offence.

Employers, of course, do have to bear in mind the sex discrimination legislation, but that is likely to be seen in the broad sense: that is, that the law does not confer upon employees the right to wear the same types of dress, but rather to conform to the same standards.

Where ethnic religious beliefs require the wearing of certain styles of dress or particular modes of appearance, those beliefs need to be accommodated unless there are very good reasons, such as safety requirements, that make it impossible.

It is not possible to specify in advance every item or style of dress that would be approved or disapproved. Therefore, all that the employer can do is to use subjective commonsense in applying rules, and, in doing so, make sure that the standards imposed are consistent for all relevant employees.

See Employment Rules Book 2.14.

3.16   Relationships

A difficult practical problem encountered from time to time, particularly in offices, is where two employees form a close personal relationship which has a harmful effect upon the work of the office (perhaps because they allow their personal relationship to intrude into the office; or it may affect other workers).

It is useful, in those circumstances, to have a contract clause which allows transfer of one or both to other departments or even to a different type of work.

Of course, such a transfer or change of job cannot be made merely because such a relationship has developed. The employer must be able to show, if necessary, that there clearly was, or was very likely to be, a detrimental effect upon work.

There is also the question of sex discrimination to consider (and maybe, in some circumstances, racial or even trade union discrimination). That is, if a transfer or job-change is patently the only solution to a difficult problem, which employee should be moved? Management is under a clear obligation to show that careful consideration is given to this question and that the criterion is without doubt solely that of the needs of the job. Moreover, indirect discrimination could result if, for example, it were shown that in such circumstances the job or procedures were so structured that one sex or the other would inevitably suffer.

See Employment Rules Book 2.15.

3.17   General restrictions, confidentiality, inventions

Generally speaking, employers are entitled to impose restrictions on employees to avoid damage to the business.

On the other hand, it would be wrong to try to lay down rules of behaviour which have nothing to do with the business.

For example, it would be perfectly proper to have a rule which barred other employment which could be prejudicial to the interests of the employer, such as where the employee engages in the same business activities of the employer. However, it would be quite wrong to impose a general bar on all outside employment unless of course in the very rare circumstance where it could be argued that any other employment would cause harm to the business.

By that same test of prejudice to business interest it could be that the employer would have the right to impose other restrictive rules.

Quite clearly an employee cannot be allowed to breach the confidence of customers. Or, for that matter, the secrets of the employer.

Also, for reasons of security, the control of the acceptance of gifts may well be desirable as may a restriction on the holding of outside directorships.

It may be appropriate for a company to claim some right to the benefits of the development of inventions or processes which have been produced with company resources.

Should it happen that an employee breaches this type of rule during employment, the employer has the power to take direct action, perhaps to recover damages through the courts or perhaps to take disciplinary action. Obviously, after employment has ended the latter remedy no longer applies.

The ability of an employer to take action against an ex-employee is somewhat restricted. If a confidence has been breached after leaving, an action for damages might well succeed. The employer can restrict the post-employment activities of an ex-employee, such as the right of that person to trade in competition, but a restriction cannot be imposed which would affect the ability of a person to earn a living. Therefore, such restrictions would be severely limited in such terms as time, geography and substance.

See Employment Rules Book 2.16, 2.17 and 2.22.

3.18 Lay-off and short-time

If lay-off or short-time working is ever necessary, the consent of the employees must be obtained, and it may be difficult to get total agreement from all employees. Therefore, if such a need is ever likely, it is better to have the employee's consent in advance by incorporating an appropriate provision in the contract of employment.

Some companies may never have the need to lay off, but it is probably wise to give the possibility advance consideration.

Lay-off occurs where the employer finds it impossible to provide the employees with work because of some circumstance outside his control, such as where there is a temporary reduction in the work-load. If this is the case it may be better to lay employees off for a short period until they will be needed again rather than to have to pay them off and thereby incur liability for notice and perhaps redundancy pay.

If it is possible to lay-off, then the employee is entitled to a guarantee payment for each day of lay-off up to a maximum of five days in any period of three months. The amount of guaranteed pay is fixed by law and is adjusted each year.

When the employee ceases to receive pay from the employer the Department of Employment will provide benefit, as for an unemployed person, although that person is still in that employment. Lay-off or short-time working does not break continuity of employment.

The length of time an employee can be kept laid off or on short-time is restricted by law and at the end of that period the employee has to be returned to full normal working or is treated as having been dismissed by reason of redundancy.

The rules surrounding lay-off and short-time are exceedingly complex and if there is ever such a need it is important to obtain further advice.

See Employment Rules Book 2.18.

3.19   Retirement

Normal retirement ages should be stated in the contract of employment.

If that is not done the employee may be able to rely upon employment protections, such as unfair dismissal rights, beyond the usual age limits.

In the absence of a contractual rule the normal retirement age will be taken to be that which can be inferred from practice.

The statutory age at which most employment protection rights cease has been 65 for a man and 60 for a woman but is to be equalised in November 1987 to a standard age of 65.

An employer may wish to adopt a normal retirement age lower than that provided by statute. Many employers have, for example, imposed a standard normal retirement age of 60 for all employees.

If that is done, the legislative rights which are dependent upon the male employee being below retiring age will cease to apply to those who reach the new age limit.

However, such an alteration may cause hardship in the individual case. Although there may be no recourse to an industrial tribunal for those who reach the altered age limit it may be that the alteration itself could be actionable if its implementation was unreasonable.

See Employment Rules Book 2.19.

3.20   Vehicles

Many employers provide certain employees with a motor car for business and private use, or the use of a commercial vehicle, van or lorry, for some private use. If the employer allows private usage then that provision becomes a contractual benefit for the employee.

Although the employer may have a rule which allows withdrawal of the right to a company car, or to allow a change in the type or make of car, it cannot be done without just cause. If withdrawal of car provision is contemplated there would have to be sound business reasons for doing so. In the same way, if changes were made in the car's model or type, to reduce its benefit value, that change would have to be justified on good business grounds. Employees usually view car provision in terms of status as well as utility, and changes can easily lead to strong grievance.

It makes sense, therefore, to have rules about car provision which are detailed as to rights and obligations. Because these can be lengthy, it may be sensible to have them as an appendix to the rules rather than have a disproportionate section in the rules themselves.

See Employment Rules Book 2.23.

3.21   Smoking

In the rare event that an entire establishment has no employee at all who smokes it would be a wise precaution to lay down a rule in the contract of employment forbidding smoking by all employees. The introduction of such a rule would probably be welcomed. If a rule was not made it might be difficult to control any existing employee who started smoking or any new recruit who was a smoker.

The usual position, however, is that in any establishment there are smokers and non-smokers. In those circumstances it would very likely be taken that the right to smoke was in-built into the contract of employment. It would therefore be unfair to impose a 'no-smoking' rule that would cause distress to those employees that smoked.

A way of overcoming this problem might be to designate certain areas, such as rest-rooms, as smoking areas and apply a 'no-smoking' rule to work areas. The main difficulty with this solution is that a heavy smoker could spend too much time away from the job.

If certain areas have to be designated non-smoking areas because of health or hazard reasons then they must obviously be so designated. However, it follows that any employees who need, for job reasons, to go into that area should have had that restriction made clear to them before being put into that job.

One method of introducing 'no-smoking' bans is to tackle the problem area by area. Where there is a work area completely staffed by non-smokers, then, with their agreement, a 'no-smoking' rule could be introduced for that one area. The ban can then be spread as and when opportunity allows.

See Employment Rules Book 2.24.

3.22   Discrimination

It is unlawful for an employer to discriminate against a person on the grounds of sex, race, colour, nationality or ethnic or national origins.

This is so at any time, whether before employment—at recruitment stage—or during employment, or indeed after.

Furthermore, the laws of sex and race discrimination apply to any person who carries out work for the employer whether a directly employed person, a self-employed person (such as a temporary worker) or the employee of someone else, say a sub-contractor.

An employer is taken to have directly discriminated where, for example, the employee is refused a job or is refused promotion on discriminatory grounds. An 'indirect' discrimination is where the employer applies some criterion which is in itself discriminatory. For example, if all or the great majority of part-time employees were women and there were some restrictions or disadvantage placed upon part-time workers, that might be held to be an indirect discrimination.

Pay equality between the sexes is also a requirement in law. Pay must be equal where women and men do like work or work that is rated as equal, or work that is of equal value. And it may well be possible for a non-employee, such as a temporary worker to claim equal pay with direct employees.

Trade union discrimination is somewhat different from sex and racial discrimination. The most important difference is that a prospective employee does not have right of redress against an employer who discriminates on trade union grounds before engagement—that is, at the recruitment stage. However, an employee acquires the right not to be discriminated against for being a member of an independent trade union, or of taking part in the activities of such union, or of seeking to join an independent union as soon as employment commences—there is no 'probationary period'.

There are, of course, special rules concerning closed shops.

See Employment Rules Book 2.25.

3.23 Security

The only recourse an employer has if an employee refuses to comply with a rule that allows a security search is to take disciplinary action. It would rarely be advisable for the employer to try to detain the employee further.

If it is felt that there are reasonable grounds for such a search, management should ensure that if the employee consents to the search that other people are present. That is, there should normally be another member of management present and the employee should be invited to ask for a fellow employee to attend.

If the employee refuses, in the presence of two or more members of management, to allow such a search, management may have to consider disciplinary action.

That action would normally follow the usual disciplinary code. In that case the employee would be made aware of the risk of dismissal for continuing refusal. Suspension would follow a continuing refusal and a disciplinary hearing would be convened. It would then be open to management to consider what evidence it had for its reasons for the search; whether it had good reason, in the light of investigations and the hearing, to believe that an offence had been committed; and whether, if it was completely satisfied of the committal of that offence, that dismissal would be the correct response.

In some establishments, admission to the worksite needs to be strictly controlled for reasons of secrecy or security. In such areas it may be sensible to require employees, by way of a rule, to be vigilant and to comply with proper controls. In many establishments it is useful to have some control or record of who is on site in case of an emergency when it can quickly be established that all are accounted for.

See Employment Rules Book 2.33.

3.24   Health and safety at work

It is a legal requirement that every employer must have a written statement of his general policy for the health and safety of his employees, and that the policy be kept up-to-date. It is also required that the policy be brought to the notice of the employees.

Although a health and safety policy is not of itself a contractual matter, the rules book is a useful vehicle for bringing it to the attention of employees. Also, a regular review of the rules would ensure that the updating of the policy is not overlooked.

The main emphasis of the legislation is upon the health and safety of employees but it should not be forgotten that the employer's duty towards non-employees such as sub-contract labour, visitors and the general public needs to be covered within a policy, as appropriate.

The health and safety requirements of individual employers will vary greatly according to the nature of the business. Obviously, what will suffice for a retail shop is not likely to be suitable for an engineering establishment. The model rule is therefore somewhat generalised but it should, with some adaptation, be suitable for, or be the basis for, most employers. The individual employer may need to seek the advice of a qualified specialist, particularly as regards working practices and equipment.

Some employers will have recognition agreements with trade unions with consequent arrangements for safety representation and safety committees and many employers who do not recognise unions have similar representation and committees. The rules that govern such representation and committees are not likely to be contractual and so the rules book is not the ideal place for them. In some establishments there will be a need for health and safety rules which apply to the generality of employees and which are contractual. For example, certain areas may have to be restricted for reasons of safety, or the wearing of protective clothing may be essential, and the consequence of breaching such rules can be set out in the rules, perhaps in the section which deals with misconduct examples.

See Employment Rules Book 2.34.

3.25   Redundancy policy

There is no legislative requirement that an employer should have a stated redundancy policy or that such a policy should be notified to employees. However, it is useful and indeed good practice to let employees know where they will stand in the event of redundancy. Furthermore, a policy which incorporates such factors as ability, absenteeism and so on may help with motivation.

The first point to note is that lay-off and short-time working can be implemented only if the employee agrees, either at the time or by having appropriate provisions in the contract of employment.

Alternative employment offers must always be a consideration before redundancy dismissal notices are issued; that is, of course, where the redundancy is short of total. If it is possible to make an offer of alternative employment it would be unfair not to do so. Indeed it might well be held to be unfair not to have examined that possibility, which does not mean that a job has to be created, merely that if a suitable one is available it must be offered.

If an employee rejects an offer of alternative employment that is patently suitable then that employee would be ineligible for redundancy pay.

Unless the redundancy is unavoidably sudden, employees should be told in advance of being given notice, and the employer should listen to any suggestions they may have to make.

Selection for redundancy, where necessary, is always difficult unless the simple continuity of employment method is used—'last-in, first-out'. Selection by merit is much more useful in that it retains the more capable employees, but this method does need to be carried out very carefully.

Selection is where some employees, but not all, within the same job-group are to be made redundant. Thus job-groups, that is groups of employees who carry out the same sort of work, need to be very well defined.

All of those within one particular job-group need to be considered by management, preferably a panel of relevant managers, and must be judged in accordance with pre-determined criteria. Where the criteria calls for subjective assessments on such matters as quality of work then that subjectivity must be tempered with objective factors, certainly length of service and perhaps attendance and so on must be considered.

Where an employer has used a method of selection in the past or has a method agreed with a trade union, that method must continue in use in the future unless there is strong evidence for a change in the selection policy.

See Employment Rules Book 2.38.

105

3.26   Grievance procedure

Employers are legally bound to have a grievance procedure and the first steps in that procedure must be notified to the employee by way of the statement of terms of employment. Any subsequent steps may be set out in a referred document such as a rules book. In small employments it may, of course, be necessary for the same person to deal with each step.

The objective of having a grievance procedure is that employees should be able to raise with management any employment-related problems before they escalate into major difficulties. Thus a grievance procedure should be looked on as a method of communication between management and employees, and its use should therefore be encouraged.

Most grievances relate to problems of pay and conditions. Therefore it is useful to have two forms of procedure; one which deals with the ordinary day-to-day problems that employees might have and which can speedily be settled, and the other which copes with the more serious disciplinary problems, such as where an employee appeals against the decision of a disciplinary panel.

All requests to use the grievance procedure should be treated seriously so that the employee can see that whatever the outcome, management has given full and careful consideration to the matter. Everything that happens relating to a grievance complaint, from the initial request through to the final decision of management, should be kept on record.

The procedure should be implemented in stages, with the initial complaint being taken up by someone close to the employee who is aware of what the problem is about, for example the immediate supervisor. At this stage the procedure should be informal so that the employee is not inhibited in taking up the matter, and also because most minor complaints can be settled without formality.

However, supervisors should understand that they have a duty not only to listen to and deal with the complaint but also to ensure that the employee is satisfied with the result, or if not that the employee is reminded of his right to take the matter further. (If he is not so reminded of these further steps the matter could lead to a claim for constructive dismissal.)

Further stages in the grievance procedure should allow for consideration by management at a more senior level than the immediate supervisor. At this more formal stage it may be required that the complaint be put in writing. However, whether this is done or not, management should hear what the employee has to say in person, and management's decision should be recorded. It is also useful to notify or confirm that decision in writing to the employee concerned.

See Employment Rules Book 2.39.

3.27 Notice

The statutory notice that an employer is required to give on termination of employment is one week after one month of employment, two weeks after two years of employment and thereafter an additional week for each complete year of employment up to a maximum of 12 weeks.

The statutory notice that an employee has to give to terminate employment is one week after one month of employment. This does not increase with length of service.

The employer and employee can agree on notice periods in excess of the statutory requirement in which case those periods become contractually binding. Neither the employer nor employee can agree on notice periods that are less than the statutory requirement.

An employee's pay is protected during the notice period. That is, if the employee is away sick or on holiday, or the employer cannot find work, then an employee must be paid as normal. But, if the employee is otherwise away without permission there is no right to pay. (Sick pay and holiday pay may be set-off.)

The right to notice and the right to be paid during notice does not apply if the employee is in fundamental breach of the contract of employment—for example, commits an act of gross misconduct, and for that reason is dismissed without notice.

If notice is not properly given the employer is in breach of contract for the amount of pay not given. In that case, if the employer gives the employee a sum which at least equals the notice pay (and any other benefits such as car-use etc.) that is due, the employee would have no right of action for recovery of that pay, that is, the employer has given 'pay in lieu'.

Unless the contract of employment provides for pay in lieu then any payment that is made in lieu of that required under the contract for the notice period is paid as damages for breach of the employee's right to paid notice. In that case the employer is not required to deduct income tax from that amount.

Note: An employee who has been dismissed by reason of redundancy has the right to take whatever time-off is reasonable during the notice period to look for other work or to seek retraining and also has the right to payment for such time off up to a maximum of two-fifths of a week's pay.

See Employment Rules Book 2.40.

3.28   Misconduct

The first action in dealing with a case of misconduct is to be as sure as possible that the misconduct did in fact take place; and that the allegation can be substantiated if necessary. That may be a simple matter or it may require some investigation.

The next step is to decide whether the problem can be dealt with simply by discussion with the person involved; or, if it is more serious, by an oral warning; or that it is so serious that a formal final warning of dismissal is required.

Whatever is decided upon, it is important that a record is kept of the action taken, and if a final warning is issued it is better that it is put in writing. It is also useful that there is some proof of the action, preferably that some other member of management was there when it was taken, and that a written warning was delivered or given in the presence of another manager.

Clearly, if a final warning is given (that is, that a repetition of the action, or inaction, will lead to dismissal) then it needs to be understood that the management is committing itself to that course of action.

If it is believed that the misconduct was so fundamental to the business that the question of dismissal must be examined without there having been any prior warnings then the procedure for gross misconduct has to be adopted. However, since dismissals without prior warning are based upon a subjective view of the gravity of the offence, it follows that the offence must be of such severity that it can be contended either that a warning was not possible because the employee could not be allowed an opportunity of repeating the offence, or that it was clear beyond doubt that a warning would have been ineffective.

Whatever course of action is decided upon it is normally inadvisable to proceed to dismissal without giving the employee an opportunity of putting his point of view to management before a final decision is taken.

See Employment Rules Book 2.41, 2.43 and 2.44.

3.29   Warnings

Before issuing any warnings it is good practice, wherever possible, to try to settle the problem in an informal way by discussing the matter with the employee, spelling out what is wrong and listening to any justifications. Although this is an informal first approach, it is as well that some note be kept of what happened, what was done by management, and the response of the employee.

If it happens that the problem continues, or was too serious to be dealt with informally, it may be that a warning will be appropriate.

Warnings may take two forms: an oral warning, usually reserved for the less serious sort of case; and the written warning, usually given where serious disciplinary proceedings are contemplated. Oral warnings should be noted for the record and copies of written warnings should be held on file.

In both cases there could be a question of proof: with the oral warning, a question not only of what was said, but also of whether it was said; and with the written warning, the question of whether it was delivered. In both cases, a witness as to delivery and content would be invaluable.

The content of the warning will, of course, reflect management's intentions. It may be that a warning may merely be intended to provoke the employee to adhere to some standard, of conduct or work-performance, and will do no more than state an objective with some sort of time period for achievement.

Or a warning may contain the threat of dismissal; then it needs to be completely unambiguous in stating the consequence of failure. The employee should be in no doubt on the matter. In the same way, if one wants an employee to conform to some stated standard one needs to spell out that standard and make the warning relate to its non-achievement; not to ask for an 'improvement' if nothing less than complete achievement is required.

All serious warnings that could lead to loss of benefit, or to dismissal, should remind the employee of the right to appeal and should say to whom such an appeal can be made.

The stage at which it will be appropriate to reach the final warning stage will depend upon the circumstances. In cases of misconduct this will usually be reached much earlier than when dealing with less clear-cut issues such as work-performance. It may be that a single act of misconduct—serious enough, but not really to be categorised as gross misconduct—will call for a final warning. Work-performance problems usually require a build-up of discussion and counselling before the warning stage is reached.

See Employment Rules Book 2.42.

3.30 Sickness and injury

A person who is working under a contract of employment is required to observe the terms of that contract. Therefore, where a contract stipulates that certain hours have to be worked it is a breach of that contract if those hours are not worked.

However, an employer is required to temper his actions in accordance with the rules of fairness, and sickness absence has to be looked at in the light of what is reasonable absence both from the view of the employer and employee.

In testing the question of fairness in relation to sickness absence one has to look to the future, albeit that past absence might indicate what the future holds. That is, it would be clearly unfair to dismiss an employee for past sickness absence if the indications were that the employee was now likely to be fit and willing to attend work.

Therefore, the employer who believes that sickness absence is likely to continue to an unacceptable degree needs some expert indication of what the future holds for that employee.

The nature of the sickness or injury may be such that the employee is likely to be absent for a continuously long period. Or, the problem may be one which causes regular or sporadic short absences. Nevertheless, if the employer feels that the level of absence is unacceptable it is necessary for him to seek a medical opinion.

It is good practice for an employer to require the employee to see a doctor of the employer's choosing for an examination. For this reason it is useful to have a provision in the contract of employment which gives the employer power to require this, although there is some obligation on the employee to do so whether or not it is contractually necessary. (A refusal by the employee to be so examined would not of itself give good ground for dismissal. In that case the employer would have to rely on whatever evidence was available, perhaps taking into account any reports from the employee's own doctor or, if no expert views were available, merely relying upon his own judgement.)

The doctor should be provided with a history of the employee's absence record and be told of the nature of the work and hours the employee is required to do. It should be made clear to the doctor that what is required is a prognosis as to the employee's future ability to work normally.

Unless there is clear medical evidence that the employee is going to continue indefinitely or for a very long period to be unable to attend normally, it would be inadvisable to dismiss. However, depending upon the evidence, it might be that the probability of a continuing medical difficulty would allow a change of job to something more compatible with the illness and the needs of the employer.

If the evidence from the employer's doctor conflicts with that of the employee's, the employer should judge whether a third medical report is called for, perhaps from a specialist in the field of the employee's illness. However, if the illness is job related, it may be said that the employer's doctor is better able to give an opinion.

A principal ingredient of fairness is consistency. It might therefore be seen to be unfair to take action against one employee on the ground of sickness absence where it is shown that other employees have received more lenient treatment in similar circumstances. It is useful, therefore, to have a procedure which triggers action when absence reaches a particular level. That does not mean that all employees have to be treated exactly the same. It may be that different jobs will allow different treatment, but it may be necessary to show that consideration was given on an equal basis. It follows from this that it is important to have good attendance records.

If it is clear that it is no longer practicable to allow an employee to continue to work in a job because of a health problem, consideration must first be given to any alternatives to dismissal. For example, where the job itself affects the employee's health (this is often so where stress or allergy is suspected) a change of job would solve the problem. Or maybe if a change would not help from a health point of view a different job would accommodate the absences.

In any case, except where it is clear that the employee will not be able to do any work of any sort, the question of offering alternative employment must be examined before proceeding to the question of dismissal. If alternative employment is taken up the new job does not necessarily have to carry the same terms of pay and conditions. There is nothing to prevent the employer from offering a job at the same salary as before, but it may be that pay policy will dictate that the salary must be that specified for the particular grade of the new job.

There is also no obligation to find a job where no such job exists. But it may be that the circumstances, particularly in the case of long-service employees, will suggest that strenuous efforts are made in this direction.

If it is apparent that there is no alternative to dismissal it is obvious that this should not be abrupt and that the employer should show compassion in the manner in which it is carried out.

There should be a period of discussion and counselling, and also the nature of the illness should be borne in mind. For example, if the illness is stress-related it is obvious that as little stress as possible is caused by the dismissal procedures.

See Employment Rules Book 2.44.

3.31   Hearings

A disciplinary procedure hearing, whether in consideration of the question of dismissal or of an appeal by an employee, is simply to enable management to ascertain all of the pertinent facts to help them reach a decision.

The employee should be made aware before the hearing of the complaints that are at issue and should be given time, preferably away from work, to consider those complaints and to get advice if he so wishes.

The timing of the hearing should be during normal working hours when the employer is able to require the attendance of the employee.

The employee should be made aware that the hearing will be held in his absence if he fails to attend without good cause. In those circumstances management can do no more than base its decision on the facts that it is able to obtain without the help of the employee. Clearly, if the employee makes any written representations they must be taken account of.

The hearing should call any person who management thinks may shed light on the matter, and hear any person the employee believes may be of help.

The employee should be allowed representation by any other fellow employee (or a full-time trade union officer if the employee is a trade union steward). A hearing is not a court where the employee is on trial and so outside representation would normally be inappropriate. However, if it is possible that the issue could involve criminal proceedings the employee should be allowed, indeed advised, to have a solicitor present, not as a representative, but merely to ensure that nothing is said that could prejudice his client in any such proceedings.

The hearing should be conducted by a senior manager, preferably someone who has not been involved in any of the previous disciplinary action, together with one or two other managers forming a panel.

The hearing should be, as its title implies, for the management to listen to everything that might be said by everyone who might have information relevant to the subject.

Accordingly, each relevant person should be allowed to speak fully, the subject employee last when he has heard what others have to say. There should be no 'trial' atmosphere and so no examination or cross-examination as such. The employee may wish to put questions about what has been said and should be allowed to do so—but not as a cross-examination. In addition the panel may want to ask questions, but not in the form of an interrogation.

Only after management is fully satisfied that it is in possession of all of the facts should a decision be taken.

See Employment Rules Book 2.45.

3.32 Suspension

Suspension from work has two principal uses: as a punishment for wrongdoing related to the business and as a period to prepare for a disciplinary hearing.

In the case of the former, it is likely that the period of suspension is not paid. In the latter, the period may be paid or not, as provided in the rules, depending upon the outcome of the hearing. In both cases the question of pay should be clarified in the rules.

Whatever the reason for suspension, there needs to be some fairly short duration limit. Clearly, the employee is in the position of not being paid by the employer and, because he is not out of employment, not being paid by the State, the matter cannot go on for very long.

Punishment suspensions, if they really are needed, should be for hours or, in severe cases, days; certainly a period extending into weeks would be difficult to justify. Moreover, the circumstances in which they may be applied should be spelled out.

Hearing suspensions would normally be a matter of days, sufficient to enable the employee to marshal arguments, facts and perhaps witnesses and, maybe, to take advice.

See Employment Rules Book 2.46.

3.33   Alternative employment

There may be many reasons why management needs to offer or should offer, alternative employment to an employee.

Reorganisation may require that an individual must change jobs, or the interests of the individual may best be served by a change of job.

In some cases the possibility of offering an employee a change of job is necessary to satisfy the rules of fairness. For example, if termination of employment is likely in cases which do not involve misconduct—say, redundancy, then the employer must look to see if there is any other employment available that the employee would be capable of doing that could be offered, thereby avoiding dismissal.

In the same way, if an employee cannot continue in his present job because of a health problem but is otherwise capable of working, or if the employee is not up to the demands of the present job, then the question of whether any other suitable jobs are available must be explored before dismissal is notified.

There is no legislative requirement that jobs must be created in those circumstances but the employer must be able to show that the possibility was examined.

The employer may wish to allow the employee to retain existing salary and benefits, but this can cause all sorts of problems. It is usually better to make the offer subject to the employee accepting the pay and conditions which the new job carries.

It is then for the employee to accept or refuse. Clearly, if an employee who was to be made redundant refused an offer of alternative employment that was suitable then there is no redundancy—suitable employment was available.

The employer may wish to make the offer subject to trial, that is, that there should be some period during which both the employer and employee will put the change in job to the test of suitability. If that is contemplated it is most important that the terms of the trial period be set out in writing for the agreement of both parties.

A trial period for redundancy pay purposes must be no more than one month. That means that if the trial fails within that month then the employee would not have lost the right to a statutory redundancy payment and the employer's right to rebate would be preserved. (Where change to a new job necessitates retraining, a trial training period of six months is permissible for redundancy pay purposes, and if necessary this period can be extended beyond six months. There again if the trial training fails, statutory redundancy pay and rebate rights are preserved.)

See Employment Rules Book 2.47.

3.34   Appeals

Appeals from managerial proceedings relating to discipline or termination of employment (as distinct from grievance appeals) should be allowed for both actions short of dismissal (perhaps the imposition of a warning or suspension) and for a decision to dismiss.

The appeal procedure can be operated before dismissal actually occurs or it may be preferable to allow post-dismissal appeals.

The appeal hearing should follow the same pattern as a disciplinary hearing. An industrial appeal should not be the same as a judicial appeal, deciding upon whether the rules had properly been applied, but should be capable of hearing any new evidence, including any facts that had emerged after dismissal in post-dismissal appeals.

It is preferable, if at all possible, that the appeal should be heard by managers who have not previously been involved.

In the case of a post-dismissal appeal it would be rare that a re-employment resulting from the appeal would break continuity of employment and it may be that such a decision should clarify this point.

Where management has discretion over suspension pay, the appeal decision should include an appropriate finding.

Verbatim records of hearings are not necessary, but clearly some record of all salient points needs to be kept.

See Employment Rules Book 2.48.

Part Four
Model Letters

Contents of Part Four

Introduction

If it becomes necessary to activate certain of the procedural rules the wording of letters, such as conduct warnings, is crucially important. Incorrect wording can lead to difficulties if the matter should go to an industrial tribunal. This Part of the Manual deals with various situations where a model can be of considerable value.

It is not recommended that stereotyped letters be sent to employees (except for letters of authorisation) and so each letter that is sent should receive individual treatment from the writer.

Letters should also not be sent without relevance to the particular circumstances. For example, circumstances may dictate that more than one warning is required; in some models the gender will need to be altered; some show alternative wording; and so on.

4.1 Job offer

A letter which is a firm offer of a job establishes a contractual obligation upon the employer to proceed with employment. That is, if the offer were withdrawn there could be action for damages.

A job-offer letter should contain the following elements:

- A reference to any previous discussions.
- The basic information about the job: pay, hours, and any other pertinent benefits such as pension, car provision and so on.
- The date of commencement and the time of starting work.
- The location for reporting and the person to report to.
- An invitation to contact the writer if there are any queries.
- A welcome to the company.

Since a letter cannot be precise as to benefits and conditions it would be as well to include a saving statement such as:

> The above is broadly in line with our discussions with you. However, the contents of this letter are subject to and, if necessary, modified by the contract documents which will be given to you on arrival. You should study those documents carefully and immediately take up with your Supervisor anything which is not clear to you.

4.2   Reference request

Dear

Re: [Prospective employee's name]

The above named, who has applied for the position of [specify position] at this Company, has given us your name for reference purposes.

We would be very grateful if you could send us under confidential cover a note of your opinion of him.[*]

It would be helpful for your reply to cover dates of service with you, duties performed and technical competence, health and attendance records, personal characteristics, reason for leaving and whether you know of any reason why he might not prove to be a suitable employee of this Company.[*]

We thank you in advance for your kind co-operation and enclose a stamped addressed envelope for your reply.

Yours sincerely

Note:
*Paragraphs to current or former employer. For a non-employer, substitute paragraphs 2 and 3 with the following:

We would be very grateful if you could send to us under confidential cover a note of your opinion of him and any other comments you think might be relevant to his employment with this Company.

4.3   Reply to request for reference (1)

Dear Sir

With reference to your enquiry regarding ex-employee I
have to inform you that the Company has a strict policy of only providing period
of employment information.

In this case, the above employee was employed by this Company
from: to:

This policy should not be taken to be any sort of comment whatsoever on the
above employee.

I am sorry that I cannot be more helpful.

Yours faithfully

Note:
You may wish to include other non-controversial information, such as job title. It should be
held in mind that subjective comments are not privileged in reference letters.

4.4   Reply to request for reference (2)

Dear Sir

With reference to your enquiry regarding ex-employee .... I have to inform you that the Company has a strict policy of not providing written reference material.

In this case, the above employee was employed by this Company
from: to: .

If you wish to obtain more information about this employee you may telephone the writer.

This policy is not to be taken as any sort of indication that the Company was in any way dissatisfied with this employee.

Yours faithfully

4.5   Reply to request for reference (3)

Dear

Re: [Subject's name]

I refer to your letter of [date] requesting a reference for the above.

I can confirm that he was employed by this Company
from: to: and has voluntarily
tendered his resignation.

As regards attendance and timekeeping I can confirm that these were all satisfactory.

During his period of employment, the Company has been of the opinion that he was a hardworking and conscientious employee and there was no reason to doubt his honesty or integrity.

We shall be sorry to lose his services and wish him well for the future.

If there is any further information you require please do not hesitate to contact me.

This information is given in the strictest confidence.

Yours sincerely

Note:
The information given in a letter of reference must be accurate. The writer cannot escape any legal obligations of what is said in such a letter. Therefore:

*   Favourable comments should be qualified as above.
*   If it is impossible to give a reference which is favourable on matters which are based upon judgements that are open to challenge, it would be better not to commit them to writing, but instead invite the recipient to a telephone discussion.

4.6   Maternity—return reminder

Dear

It is now more than 49 days following your confinement and under current legislation you are required to advise the Company within 14 days of receiving this letter whether or not you still intend to return to work during or at the end of the maternity absence period.

According to law, we have to state that if you do not reply in writing within 14 days of receipt of this letter you will forfeit your right to return.

Should you decide to return to work you are reminded that at least 21 days before the date of your return you are required to advise the Company in writing of the proposed return date.

For your information your maternity leave period ends:

Yours sincerely

To: Personnel Manager

From:

I wish to notify you that I intend/do not intend* to return to work.

Signed: Date:

* Please delete as applicable

4.7   Redundancy—notification to employee

Dear

This is to confirm our discussion on [date] with regard to the question of redundancy.

As you are aware from that meeting it appears that your redundancy is inevitable.

That being so we intend to follow our customary/agreed redundancy procedure, a copy of which is attached.[*]

As was explained to you, that procedure means that you are entitled to put to management anything which you feel might have a bearing on the matter. That includes any suggestion on your part for any change to the procedure itself.

In particular, if you feel that there is any way by which your redundancy can be avoided or in any way handled differently you are invited to say so now.

We shall ourselves continue to examine the matter and if we find that there is any alternative that is reasonably open to us we shall let you know.

It is with considerable regret that we have to take this course, and we do wish to make sure that all possible avenues are explored. Therefore, anything you wish to put forward at this stage will receive careful consideration.

Yours sincerely

Note:
*If this is the first occurrence of redundancy within the organisation and you have no agreed procedure, amend this paragraph to:

That being so, we intend to follow our redundancy policy, a copy of which is attached.

Also, in the next paragraph, alter 'procedure' to 'policy' throughout.

4.8   Redundancy—notice

Dear

It is with considerable regret that we now have to confirm your redundancy.

Following our recent discussions with you and in accordance with our customary/agreed[*] redundancy policy we therefore have to give notice that your employment with us will terminate on .... by reason of redundancy.

This notice is inclusive of . . . weeks of notice to which you are entitled under your contract of employment.

Your attention is drawn to your statutory entitlement to take a reasonable amount of time off work during this notice period for the purposes of seeking new employment or for making arrangements for any retraining. If you do wish to take such time off you should ask permission from your Supervisor.

Any time off that is granted for these purposes will be paid/The first two days of any time off that is granted for these purposes will be paid[**].

We thank you for your service to the Company and we sincerely hope that you will soon find other employment.

Yours sincerely

Notes:
1   *If this is the first occurrence of redundancy within the organisation delete the words 'customary'/'agreed'.
2   **The statutory right to take time off during a period of redundancy notice is to take whatever time off is reasonable. That means that time off should be allowed to whatever extent the employee requires provided it does not unreasonably interfere with work

arrangements. The statutory right to pay for such time off is for two days only. However, you may of course pay in excess of that.

3   You should include in this letter or in a follow-up letter details about leaving arrangements. That is, any redundancy pay that is due, pension, any loans repayable, etc.

4.9 Offer of alternative employment with trial period in redundancy cases

Dear

As you are aware from our recent discussions the position you have had with the Company is no longer open for the reasons explained.

Normally, this would have led to your redundancy. However, as was explained to you we are able to offer you what we believe is suitable alternative employment.

We are pleased that you have agreed to give this new post a trial and accordingly set out the terms of the post below.

As was explained to you, you are entitled by law to a trial period of one month during which time if it is felt that the new post is not one which is suitable you will revert to the previous position. In that case, of course, it appears at this moment that there would be no alternative to redundancy.

It is necessary that you formalise acceptance of this trial period by signing and returning one copy of this letter before commencement of the period.

Terms:

Trial period commences: [date],   and concludes: [date]

Yours sincerely

I, [name], accept a trial period as above. It is understood that this acceptance does not in any way prejudice my rights in relation to the redundancy pay legislation. I further accept that if the trial is successful these terms will amend my contract of employment immediately on the expiry of the trial period.

Signed: Date:

Note:
It is important that all differences between the previous and proposed contracts be stated above. These proposals should have been fully discussed with the employee before this letter is sent.

4.10 Conduct warning

Dear

This is a formal warning regarding [for example: your timekeeping; your standard of dress; your negligence in respect of ....; etc.]

You have been spoken to before about this and I now have to tell you that any further failure by you in this regard will be treated as a disciplinary matter which, subject to the process of the Disciplinary Rules, will be regarded as justifying your dismissal.[*]

If you are of the view that I am in any way being unfair in issuing you with this warning you are entitled to appeal in accordance with the Disciplinary Rules against its issue and retention on your personnel file.

I sincerely hope that you will respond to this warning and that no further action in this regard will be necessary.

Yours sincerely

Note:
*Retain this paragraph if the employee has been spoken to before on this matter and ensure that you have a record of such discussions.

Normally, there should be discussion with an employee to try to resolve the matter of complaint and only if the employee subsequently fails should a final warning be given. However, there may be cases where the offence is serious enough (short of being classified as gross misconduct) to warrant a final warning on a first offence.

A final warning should normally be a confirmation of a personal interview with the employee.

4.11 Conduct—confirmation of suspension and notification of hearing

Dear

This is to confirm that you were today suspended from work under the Company's Disciplinary Procedure.

In accordance with that procedure you are required to attend a disciplinary hearing at [time] on [date].

The reason for your suspension and the matters that will be put to you at that hearing, for you to reply to are:

These are serious charges which could lead to your dismissal and so I am enclosing a copy of the Disciplinary Procedure. It is suggested that you examine this carefully so that you will be fully aware of the procedure and your rights and obligations under it. If there is anything that is not completely clear to you please let me know immediately.

Should there be any good reason why you cannot attend the hearing as specified above you must let me know immediately otherwise the hearing will be held in your absence.

If there are any fellow employees who you think should attend to give information material to the matter of issue you should let me know immediately in order that arrangements can be made for their attendance.

If you believe that you are entitled to have a legal representative present at the hearing in accordance with the Hearings rule it would be helpful if you would let me know in advance and for you to show that person the Disciplinary Rules.[*]

Yours sincerely

Note:
*This paragraph should only be included where there is a possibility of criminal proceedings arising from the cause of the suspension.

4.12 Conduct—confirmation of result of hearing: dismissal

Dear

This is to confirm the findings of the Disciplinary Hearing held today on the matters which were put to you.

Having heard all that management could ascertain was relevant to the issue, and in particular what you had to say, it is the decision of management that the only course that is appropriate in the circumstances is that you should be dismissed.

Accordingly, your dismissal is with immediate effect as of this date/effective as from [date] when you were informed[*]

and is therefore without notice or pay in lieu of notice[*]

with ... weeks' pay in lieu of notice[*]

with ... weeks' notice to terminate on [date][*]

although you are to serve a period of notice, during that period you will still be in our employ and will therefore be subject to attend work at any time during notice if so required[*]

It is the further decision of management that the period of suspension will/will not[*] be paid.

You are reminded that you have the right under the Disciplinary Procedure to appeal against this decision and that if you wish to do so you must notify me of that appeal in writing within ... days.

In the event that you do not so appeal, all outstanding monies and employment documents due to you on termination will be sent to you as soon as it can be arranged.[**]

Yours sincerely

Notes:
1   *Delete as applicable.
2   **Where termination is immediate.

4.13 Conduct—confirmation of result of hearing: no dismissal

Dear

This is to confirm the findings of the Disciplinary Hearing held today on the matters which were put to you.

Having heard all that management could ascertain was relevant to the issue, and in particular what you had to say, it is the decision of management that the course of action that is appropriate in the circumstances is that you should not be dismissed.

However, you are hereby warned that if management has any further need of complaint against you in this regard, it may be that the only course of action open will be your dismissal/immediate dismissal[*]/However, you must be aware that management takes a serious view of the matters put to you and dismissal was only averted in the light of the mitigating circumstances. Therefore, the final warning that was issued to you on .... still remains valid[*].

It is the further decision of management that the period of suspension will/will not[*] be paid.

You are reminded that you have the right under the Disciplinary Procedure to appeal against this decision and that if you wish to do so you must notify me of that appeal in writing within . . . days.

Yours sincerely

Note:
*Delete as applicable.

4.14   Work-performance warning (1)

Dear

As you are aware from the previous discussions we have had about your work-performance with regard to

[State here the nature of the problem]

management is very concerned that you do not appear to be able to respond to these discussions.

It is with reluctance therefore that I have to tell you that it is felt that this failure on your part cannot be allowed to continue. If it should be that you are unable within the next few weeks[*] to demonstrate that you can achieve the required standard, management will have to examine the possibility that you cannot continue in your present position.

If you are of the view that I am in any way being unfair in this regard you are invited to discuss the matter further with me and/or to appeal against this warning in accordance with the Disciplinary Rules.

I sincerely hope that you will be able to respond satisfactorily and that this matter need go no further.

Yours sincerely

Notes:
1   *The time period will depend upon the nature of the work.
2   It is, of course, important that you can substantiate the problem and, if possible, that previous discussions with the employee demonstrate the problem. Records of previous discussions should be available.

4.15   Work-performance warning (2)

Dear

It is with considerable regret that I have to confirm to you my view that you still appear to be unable to achieve a satisfactory standard of work-performance as referred to in my previous letter dated ....

In the light of that I can see no other course open to management but to examine the question of your continuing in your present position.

Therefore, I invite you to discuss this problem with me on [time and date] at [place] with a view to deciding your future employment, and it may be that you will be able to contribute your views on the matter.

I am sincerely sorry that this course of action is now necessary.

You are, of course, entitled at this stage, as at any other, to make whatever representation you feel proper, both to me and to my superiors, either informally, or to make a formal appeal in accordance with the Employment Rules.

Yours sincerely

Note:
This letter should be given personally where possible, but the employee should not be invited to discuss its contents until he has had time for consideration.

4.16 Work-performance—notification of hearing

Dear

As you are aware from our previous discussions, it is my view that your work-performance is such that it is no longer practicable to keep you in your present position.

Therefore, management has decided that in accordance with the rules you should be given an opportunity of putting your views to a panel of managers.

If it is found by that panel that you should not continue in your present position full consideration will be given to such questions as transfer to a different job more suitable to your capabilities and you should be prepared to give your views on such possibilities.

However, it should be made clear that if that is the finding of the panel, and if there are no practicable alternatives, termination of your employment will be the only possible course then open.

You are therefore required to attend a panel hearing at [time] on [date].

In order that you may be able to give full consideration to the matter it is suggested that you take paid leave of absence from now until the hearing.

Enclosed is a copy of the relevant procedures which you should read carefully. If there is anything that is unclear you should let me know immediately.

If there is any good reason why you cannot attend the hearing you must let me know immediately otherwise the hearing will be held in your absence.

If there are any other fellow employees who you think should attend to give information material to the issue you should let me know immediately in order that arrangements can be made for their attendance.

Yours sincerely

4.17   Sickness authorisation

Dear

In accordance with your contract of employment it is required that you attend for a medical examination by the Company's doctor, [name of doctor], at [place] on [time and date] in order that he can provide us with a report on your health.

If it is impossible for you to attend on that date you should let me know immediately, stating the reason and, where appropriate, when you will be free to so attend.

It may be helpful to the doctor to be able to obtain relevant information from your own doctor. Therefore, you are asked to complete the authorisation below to facilitate this. If that authorisation is not provided our doctor will have to provide us with a report based upon his findings alone.

Yours sincerely

To: [employee's name]

Please return this authorisation immediately to the Personnel Department.

I hereby give you my permission to allow the Company's doctor to make contact with my doctor and any other medical practitioner I am currently consulting to obtain any relevant medical information.

My doctor's name is:

His surgery address is:

His telephone number is:

4.18   Sickness termination

Dear

Thank you for attending the meeting yesterday/allowing us to visit you yesterday[*] regarding the unfortunate circumstances of your illness.

As you are aware from the previous discussions we have had on this subject we have been concerned for some time in this regard and had reached the position where we felt that it had become necessary to take a decision about your continued employment with the Company.

In the light of all that we are able to ascertain it seems clear to us that the only course of action that is appropriate is that we have to terminate your employment.

From our discussions you will know that it is with considerable regret, and only after long deliberation, that we have felt bound to come to this decision.

If after reflection you feel that this decision is at all wrong or unfair please do not hesitate to make your views known to .... Obviously, in that case you should do so as quickly as possible so that [name] can take any action which [name] thinks is proper.

As you will be aware you are entitled to ... weeks of notice and therefore your employment will terminate on: , and of course, the period of notice will be paid/It appears to us that the best advantage to you in these unfortunate circumstances is that you be given payment in lieu of notice[*].

All outstanding monies and employment documents due to you will be given to you on termination/are being sent to you[*].

[It may be appropriate to include personal good wishes etc.]

Yours sincerely

Note:
*Delete as applicable.

4.19   Offer of alternative employment

Dear

We are pleased that you have accepted the change[s] to your contract of employment which were the subject of our recent discussions.

It is therefore necessary for us to formalise the appropriate amendment to your contract of employment as follows:

[enter details]

The implementation date for change is .... and accordingly your contract of employment is amended as above from that date.

It is necessary that before implementation of these terms both parties consent in writing. As you will see we have signed acceptance below and you should sign one copy of this letter and return it as soon as possible, retaining the other copy for your records.

Yours sincerely

The contract of employment of [name] is amended as follows from [date]. [Enter details]

I, [name], accept the above amendment of my contract of employment.

Signature: Date:

The above amendment of the contract of employment of [name] is accepted on behalf of the Company.

Signed:

Position: Date:

Note:
It is important that the above changes should have been fully explained to the employee, with oral acceptance, before this letter is sent.

Part Five
Law Check

Contents of Part Five

Introduction

This part of the Manual deals with the rights, obligations and restrictions imposed by employment legislation on employers and employees.

Only those rights which are actionable through industrial tribunals are dealt with here.

All of the rights provided for in employment law are subject to restrictions of some sort. That is, that for an employee to be able to obtain redress from an industrial tribunal certain conditions have to be satisfied.

Some of those conditions relate to length of service. For example, an employee must have been continuously employed by the employer for at least one month before having the right to be given a statutory notice period to terminate the employment. Other conditions relate to age, hours of work and so on. Each of these main conditions is dealt with in this section.

If an employee makes a claim which appears to be excluded by one of the restrictions an industrial tribunal will consider the question of its jurisdiction at a preliminary hearing.

Note:
'Employment' means continuous employment with the same employer. 'Discrimination' includes dismissal.

5.1   Eligibility

Before engagement

It is unlawful to discriminate against a prospective employee on the grounds of race or sex (including the self-employed or the employees of another employer who do any work for you).

After engagement

It is unlawful to discriminate against an employee at any time on the grounds of race or sex (including the self-employed or the employees of another employer who do any work for you). Except where there is a closed shop agreement in force an employee has the right not to be discriminated against at any time after engagement for being a member of, or seeking to become a member of, or for taking part in the legitimate activities of an independent trade union.

One month

An employee with one month of employment is entitled to:

- A guarantee payment if laid off.
- Notice to terminate employment and pay during notice. (Notice entitlement increases according to length of service.)

Thirteen weeks

An employee is entitled to be given, by his employer, within 13 weeks of engagement a statement of those main terms and conditions of his employment that are specified by law.

Six months

An employee with six months or more employment who has been dismissed has the right to be given, within 14 days of so requesting, a written statement of the reasons for the dismissal.

One year

An employee with one year of employment who was engaged before 1 June 1985 is entitled not to be unfairly dismissed. (Except where during the whole of that person's employment the number of employees has not exceeded 20 when the qualifying period is two years.)

Two years

An employee with two years of employment is entitled to:

- The right not to be unfairly dismissed (if engaged after 31 May 1985).
- Maternity pay and to take time off work for maternity.
- Redundancy pay if dismissed by reason of redundancy.
- Take reasonable time off during a redundancy notice period to look for other employment or to seek retraining and to be paid for such time off up to two-fifths of a week's pay.

Specific task contracts

An employee who is engaged to carry out a specific task which is not expected to last more than 12 weeks is not entitled to a guarantee payment if laid off during that 12-week period and is not entitled to receive notice to terminate the employment. However, if it should happen that employment continues beyond 12 weeks then those rights will subsist and, of course, other employment rights will accrue with passage of time.

Short fixed-term contracts

An employee who is engaged on a fixed-term contract which has a duration of 12 weeks or less has no entitlement to a guarantee payment if laid off during that period. However, if employment continues beyond the fixed term the contract of employment will revert to being a normal contract with all of the entitlements.

Fixed-term contracts

An employee employed under a fixed-term contract of one year or more, where that contract contains a provision excluding the right to complain of unfair dismissal at termination of the contract, has no such right if the contract ends merely because of its expiry. Nor does such an employee have the right to seek an order of interim relief (an order that the employment shall be continued pending a full tribunal hearing) if dismissed on trade union grounds.

An employee employed under a fixed-term contract of two years or more, where that contract contains a provision excluding the right to a statutory redundancy payment at termination of the contract, has no such redundancy pay right if the contract ends merely because of its expiry.

Employment outside Great Britain

An employee who is engaged in work wholly or mainly outside Great Britain (unless that person ordinarily works in Great Britain and the work overseas is for the same employer) is not entitled to the right to have a statement of terms at engagement or the right to notice or notice pay at termination of employment.

Furthermore if, under that contract, the employee ordinarily works outside Great Britain, there is no entitlement to:

- an itemised pay statement;
- guarantee pay if laid off;
- maternity pay and time off;
- time off for public duties or for trade union reasons;
- time off during redundancy notice;
- protection with regard to trade union membership;
- complain of unfair dismissal;
- a written statement of the reason for dismissal.

An employee is excluded from the right to have a statutory redundancy payment if, on the date of dismissal, the employee is outside Great Britain (except where the employee ordinarily works in Great Britain and the work overseas is for the same employer). If, however, the employee does ordinarily work outside Great Britain, but on the date of dismissal the employee is in Great Britain on the employer's instructions his right to any redundancy pay is preserved.

Retirement

A woman who attains the age of 60 and a man who attains the age of 65 loses the right to have a statutory redundancy payment.

An employee who reaches the normal retiring age for a person employed by a company loses the right to complain of unfair dismissal. If the company has no 'normal' retiring age then that right is lost at the age of 60 for a woman (65 from November 1987) and 65 for a man.

Part-time employment

Part-time employees do not have the right to:

- a statement of terms at engagement;
- an itemised pay statement;
- guarantee pay if laid off;
- maternity pay and time off;
- time off for public duties or for trade union reasons;
- time off during redundancy notice;
- notice or notice pay;
- complain of unfair dismissal;
- redundancy pay;
- a written statement of the reasons for dismissal.

A 'full-time' employee for this purpose is someone who is normally employed for 16 or more hours weekly; or any employee with five years or more of continuous employment who is normally employed for eight or more hours weekly.

Moreover, if an employee's hours are reduced to below 16 a week, but more than seven, that employee retains 'full-time' status for the ensuing 26 weeks, notwithstanding that the period of employment is less than five years.

Check:

Has the employee been continuously employed for five years or more?

If YES: Are the employee's normal working-hours eight or more a week?

 If YES: the employee is 'full-time'
 If NO: the employee is not 'full-time'

If NO: Are the employee's normal working hours 16 or more a week?

 If YES: the employee is 'full-time'
 If NO: have the employee's normal hours been reduced from 16 or more, to less than 16 but more than seven a week in the past 26 weeks?
  If YES: the employee is 'full-time'
  If NO: the employee is not 'full-time'

Notes:
1 The above rights are statutory rights only; for example, an employee might have a contractual right to notice above and beyond that specified by statute which is enforceable at law.
2 Lay-off (where guarantee pay arises) is not an automatic right for employers; an employee can only be laid off with the agreement of the employee, either at the time or by prior inclusion in the contract of employment.

5.2 Rights

Main statutory rights

1 To have a written statement of terms of employment.
2 Not to be discriminated against on grounds of sex or race.
3 Of both sexes to have equal work opportunities and pay and terms of employment.
4 To have a written statement of pay deductions.
5 Not to be kept laid off or on short time beyond specified limits.
6 To guaranteed pay when laid off.
7 To be paid for certain maternity leave.
8 To take time off work for maternity reasons.
9 To take time off work for public duties.
10 To take time off work for trade union duties.
11 Not to be discriminated against during employment or at termination of employment on trade union grounds.
12 To notice at termination of employment.
13 To pay during notice.
14 To time off during redundancy notice.
15 Not to be unfairly dismissed.
16 Not to be dismissed for specified reasons, e.g. pregnancy.
17 To a redundancy payment if dismissed by reason of redundancy.
18 To seek a continuation of contract (interim relief) if dismissed on trade union grounds.
19 Of recognised trade unions to seek redundancy protective awards.
20 Of recognised trade unions to be consulted about redundancy.

All of the above rights are subject to qualification.

Principal exclusions from rights

Excluded	From rights:
Less than one month of employment	6, 12, 13
Less than 13 weeks of employment	1
Less than one year of employment	15*
Less than two years of employment	7, 8, 14, 17
Part-time employees	1, 4, 6, 7, 8, 9, 10, 12, 13, 14, 15, 17
Employment outside Great Britain	1, 4, 6, 7, 8, 9, 10, 12, 13, 14, 15, 17, 18

*This period is two years where, during the period of employment of the dismissed person, the number of employees in that employment did not exceed 20.

150

Appendix: main Acts of Parliament relating to employment

Terms and Conditions of Employment Act 1959
Equal Pay Act 1970
Trade Union and Labour Relations Act 1974
Health and Safety at Work etc Act 1974
Sex Discrimination Act 1975
Employment Protection Act 1975
Race Relations Act 1976
Employment Protection (Consolidation) Act 1978
Employment Act 1980
Transfer of Undertakings (Protection of Employment) Regulations 1981
Employment Act 1982
Social Security and Housing Benefits Act 1982 (statutory sick pay)
Employment Act 1984
Wages Act 1986

Index